COLLOQUIAL ARABIC

WITH NOTES ON THE VERNACULAR SPEECH OF EGYPT, SYRIA, AND MESOPOTAMIA, AND AN APPENDIX ON THE LOCAL CHARACTERISTICS OF ALGERIAN DIALECT

By

DE LACY O'LEARY, D.D.

AUTHOR OF

Arabic Thought and its Place in History

How Greek Science Passed to the Arabs

LONDON

ROUTLEDGE & KEGAN PAUL LTD.

BROADWAY HOUSE: CARTER LANE, E.C.4.

Twelfth impression
1958

Made and printed in Great Britain by
William Clowes and Sons Ltd., London and Beccles

CONTENTS

PREFACE

THIS manual aims at providing an easy guide to the colloquial Arabic of Egypt, Syria, and Mesopotamia. There are differences of usage and pronunciation between those several parts, but they are differences in detail, not separate languages, and there seems no good reason why they may not be treated reasonably together provided that reference is made, as here, to those differences. To a very large extent those countries have had a common cultural life with close and constant intercourse, and so the language which has served as a medium of that intercourse has a very large common factor. But we are here using " colloquial " to mean the language of ordinary speech which serves as the general medium of communication between various districts and different classes and groups of men. Beneath this common speech in general use there are many local dialects, just as there are in the various parts of England, and at first it is not always easy to understand the speech of a man who uses a dialect of marked character, a difficulty which also may happen in many parts of England. Certainly these local dialects have points of great philological interest, and are well worth accurate observation and record, but it seems fair and reasonable to treat " colloquial Arabic " as the current speech in general use amongst those who have perhaps received some measure of education, and whose intercourse is not confined to a small group of fellow villagers. In these pages, therefore, although note is frequently taken of the peculiarities of local dialects which will be heard, the aim has been, not to reproduce any one of those marked dialects in its entirety but to set forth the type of speech which will be intelligible generally throughout the area stated, and will serve as a basis for accurate observation of a local dialect if occasion arises to render that desirable.

It has been assumed that the learner is endeavouring to teach himself, not that this is an ideal way or in any sense to be commended, but it is reasonable that a manual should be self-explanatory to such a degree that it is not necessary to ask a teacher what it means. The actual teacher will, no doubt, supplement or rearrange its contents, for in every case a teacher has his own ideas and his own system, but it still remains a more satisfactory method that the book, so far as it goes, should be written with the aim of explaining itself as fully as possible, and for this end it may often, as here, state in detail simple facts which the reader already knows: but it seems wiser not to assume that knowledge lest some, a very small minority no doubt, may have forgotten or never have known certain elementary facts about language. This is the more necessary, in the writer's opinion, because some readers will, in all probability, work with native teachers, whose training has been on lines so different from those of an English education that the learner will not easily recognize principles which he had put before him in his school days in quite different form.

A school of teachers of modern languages has for some years past aimed at what is known as the "direct method", endeavouring to teach the adult a foreign language by means similar to those used by children when learning their own. Indirectly their work has certainly freshened our current methods of teaching, and has helped to break down conventional systems which have shown limitations, but it hardly seems that this direct method can be applied generally; normally we have not the years and leisure at our disposal to learn a new speech in the slow way we learned our own, guidance as to general principles and observation of tendencies which hold good in a number of cases shortens and simplifies our work, and thus we are brought back to a study of grammar, not the learning of arbitrary rules which the learned have laid down as the literary standard, but simply the observation and statement of the general principles which ease and shorten our work. It is the fashion to call these statements "rules", but they are more properly regarded as generalizations designed to shorten and simplify the student's work. As far as possible these have been expressed in the simplest and least technical language, and are abridged as much as is consistent with an intelligible form: even the adult learner looks with jealous eye at the theoretical statements he is called upon to master. Occasionally reference has been made to other dialects and to historical principles, but this has been done only where it serves to show that there is a reason for a "rule" which otherwise would appear entirely arbitrary; it is easier to remember something which is shown to have a reason than one which is stated without explanation.

Many modern language teachers are averse from the use of translation as a method of teaching. Their protests certainly have served to correct some of the defects which have long defaced the use of translation for this purpose, but it seems, on the whole, that a certain measure of translation can be used conveniently in teaching. It shows how to put together sentences and arrange them in consecutive speech, and so how to set forth a train of thought naturally in the foreign medium and to observe the general tone and "genius" of its methods. In Arabic, unfortunately, we are not able to make much use of this method as the literary language, apart from the fact that it is written in a different script, has a form very far removed from that of the colloquial. At the end of this manual (Appendix III) we give one short

Sura of the Qur'an, transcribed in Roman letters, because phrases from that particular Sura, which corresponds with the "Lord's Prayer" of Christians, are frequently heard in ordinary speech: there, as in poetry and the classical language generally, the short vowel endings of the cases and moods will be observed, things unknown to the colloquial. Probably the reader will gather that the step forward to a knowledge of the classical or literary language would not be so formidable as he might have anticipated, and this will perhaps encourage him to go forward to a study of Arabic literature, classical or modern. Amongst Muslims generally the culture derived from classical Arabic is highly esteemed, and this renders it much to be desired, though later it will no doubt appeal for its own sake. The ability to quote some poetic passages or to cite ancient proverbs on appropriate occasion will open access to precincts otherwise closed, and provoke esteem such as in this country given only to high rank or great wealth. This manual, however, claims only to deal with the colloquial, and so, from the circumstances of the case, it is impossible to introduce the pupil to the study of literature.

Effort has been made to render the form of this manual as easy as possible to the unaided learner. Sounds might be represented more accurately by the help of diacritical points or of a special type such as is used in Canon Gairdner's excellent manual of Egyptian Arabic. But these methods, so useful for representing the shades of local dialect, are rather deterrent to the average learner, who wants his task put before him in the easiest form possible. The only diacritical signs employed are the marks used to denote the long vowels, and these are in so general use that they can hardly be considered as a new thing to learn. The emphatic consonants are distinguished by the use of dots beneath the letters. The official system recently set forth for use in the British administrative area is by no means satisfactory, as it takes no note of the difference between the ordinary and emphatic consonants, and failing to make this distinction would be fatal in colloquial use, as there are many instances where words differ in meaning according to whether an emphatic is, or is not, used. It has apparently been planned to suit the typewriter of western manufacture. It has seemed best to make only a very sparing use of capital letters. The use of capitals is a late mediæval invention of doubtful value, and it is not clear that Arabic would gain by the introduction of this custom. Similarly, only slight use has been made of the extremely artificial and questionable system of punctuation now in vogue in English; this also is a comparatively recent introduction, and the system which is now generally adopted and which some people desire to enforce as "correct" is an extremely mechanical one, which has but little to say in its favour. Of course, Arabic, written in its own script, has neither capitals nor any save a very rudimentary punctuation, and, whilst it is convenient for anyone learning the colloquial to have the Arabic transcribed into European script, it does not follow that it would be made more intelligible by introducing those peculiarities which adorn or deface modern English.

The transcription endeavours to represent fairly the speech of the educated Arabic-speaking people, and the system of transliteration gives approximate English sounds, but these will not be found always observed consistently, especially after the first few lessons. There is no standardized system of transliteration, and Arabic script itself does not represent the actual colloquial. In these pages the long vowels (not final) and diphthongs, as well as most of the consonants, are transliterated consistently in accordance with the values given in Chapter I, but the short vowels, especially short a, as there stated, frequently modifies to e and to i, so that it is sometimes nearer truth to transcribe it as e or i, in reality it has rather the indeterminate sound of the -a- in " beggar ": this variation ought not to cause much trouble, variants a, e, i, will be heard in the colloquial in the rendering of the same word, not merely as differences of dialect but even as differences between different social groups in the same town: a strict consistency in rendering those sounds would lead the learner to suppose that there was an absolutely fixed standard and that would be to mislead him. So u short may often be short o and it is as well to face from the first that those short vowel sounds are not finally fixed. Of course they should be represented quite correctly as spoken if we are making a study of a particular dialect, but in that case our results will not hold good for places only a few miles distant. In the following pages, as already said, we are not aiming at the dialect of a special locality but the current speech generally intelligible amongst the educated and partly educated of Egypt, Syria, and 'Iraq. In the case of the consonants matters are rather different: the main variations in the aspirate dentals and in the g and q sounds are clearly defined dialectal differences and these are stated in detail. But even here there is some inconsistency admitted: normally " dh " sounds in Egypt and Syria as " d ", but on occasion we have rendered it as " z ": in fact that happens when the word has come through Persian influence, directly or via Turkish, or else is a word more or less technically theological in its character and so represents " nahwy ", i.e. the artificial attempt of the educated to reproduce the true Arab sounds. Thus " dhikr " = " remembering " ought to be " dikr " in Egypt, but used of the religious exercise of the darwishes which has become so popular a form of devotion it is invariably called " zikr ", the reason being that the darwishes and their religious exercises were introduced into Egypt by Saladin and so came with a Persian-Turkish origin. In using vocabularies, examples, etc., the reader should remember that short a, e, i, often interchange and it is not necessary to adhere strictly to one of these unless, of course, in contact with a "throat" sound when the true "a" must be retained: so I can write al-gamal, el-gemel, il-gemel and can hear all these various renderings in use.

When all is done, however, the representation of phonology in the printed text is no more than approximate: I do not believe that the learner can ever get the sounds correctly from written symbols, nor even from a teacher, nor from gramophone records: it cannot be learned until he sojourns in the midst of an Arabic-speaking community and hears Arabic spoken all round him in every different tone of voice and without any conscious effort to reach a foreigner. All that can be hoped is that the book-taught pupil will then get hold of the language more rapidly and more correctly than one who has not had such preparation.

Such a manual as this present is written that it may be thrown aside in due course, when the usages of colloquial speech have become second nature to the learner and its modest vocabularies are replaced by an abundant supply of words appropriate to the particular needs of his occupation. But until that much to be desired consummation it will often be necessary to refer back to statements of principles and to vocabularies: for this reason pains have been taken to classify and index the matter and to classify the vocabularies in a way easy for reference. The average adult who learns a thing does not remember it and has to refresh his memory a good many times until at length the information clings and reference is needed no more. The utility of such a manual very largely depends upon easiness of reference.

Finally, a word of advice as to further studies. For grammar the learner cannot do better than use the *Alfiyya* of Ibn Malik and Ibn 'Aqil's commentary on it: the work has been in use for centuries and the text itself has difficulties, but nothing, I venture to suggest, can give quite such good results if steadily used with the help of a good native teacher or with Ibn 'Aqil's commentary and patient work. A scientific knowledge of grammar according to modern European standards means, of course, a comparative study of Arabic and some other Semitic language or languages. Literature implies either the classical material which will be found outlined in such works as Nicholson's *Literary History of the Arabs*, or modern material which has been produced in considerable abundance, some of it, such as the poetry of Shawki Bey, of the highest merit. Quite of recent years special attention has been given to the special forms of local dialects and some of the material produced as a result of such study is deserving of careful attention: of this class we may note the admirable dialogues contained in Gairdner's *Egyptian Colloquial Arabic* and the stories published by Miss Padwick in the *Bull. of the School of Oriental Studies*, III, 3, pp. 421–446, both dealing with Lower Egyptian and Dulac's *Contes Arabes* gives stories in the dialect of Upper Egypt, and Malinjoud in the *Journal Asiatique* for April–June, 1924, gives some excellent specimens of the dialect of Damascus. This, however, is a subject in which much remains still to be done.

DE LACY O'LEARY.

COLLOQUIAL ARABIC

CHAPTER I

PRELIMINARY

THE object of the following pages is to supply a convenient manual of colloquial Arabic as used in Egypt, Syria (including Palestine), and 'Iraq or Mesopotamia, with some reference to North Africa. There are differences of detail distinguishing the languages of these countries, but those differences are small when compared with the material common to them all, and it is unpractical to treat each dialect as though it were a separate language. As occasion arises attention has been drawn to the chief points of difference, and sometimes reference is made to the dialectal characteristics of Oman and of Western Arabic (Morocco, Algeria, and Tunis), but no effort has been made to give complete guidance to those other dialects. The area in view in these pages forms a rough semi-circle round the desert which forms the northern part of Arabia, the home of the Arabic language, and the whole of this area has had a unity of cultural life throughout the Muslim period, the resultant intercourse producing a community of speech in spite of distinctive local differences.

It must be understood, however, that there are limitations to our use of the word "colloquial"; it is not so used as to include each type of local dialect. A person who learned colloquial English would hardly expect to know in detail the dialects prevailing in the various rural districts, many of which would be very difficult to the average educated Englishman. Local dialect is a highly specialized study which has only received serious attention of quite recent years, and, whilst it is useful to point out local peculiarities, it is not usually expedient to learn a language in strict conformity with the speech of the peasant population in one particular district. In any case, the specialized study of local dialect may properly be regarded as supplementary to a general knowledge of the language as spoken over the wider area. To a very large extent the Arabic of Lower Egypt, Palestine, and Syria shows a common character, that of Upper Egypt inclines more towards the speech of the desert Arabs, and, in some respects, to that of North Africa, whilst the Arabic of 'Iraq is closer to the parent speech from which all have been derived.

A satisfactory colloquial knowledge implies four things, (i) a sufficient number of words, (ii) the right manner of pronouncing them, (iii) the necessary modifications of those words as they are grouped together, e.g. the different persons of the verb, the formation of the plural, etc., and (iv) the correct arrangement of words in intelligible sentences. Of these (i) the formation of a vocabulary is mainly a matter of memory supplemented by reading and by conversation. This present manual contains a selection of the commonest words which form a fair basis for ordinary conversation, but these should be supplemented by the use of a dictionary and by the compilation of special vocabularies according to special needs, e.g. technical terms of medicine, engineering, for commercial purposes, etc.

(ii) The pronunciation of a foreign language is always a leading difficulty and this cannot be learned from books, hardly even from a teacher, however good. The only satisfactory method is to mix in intercourse with those who speak the language; in some mysterious way the ear co-operates with the tongue, and so one begins to tune one's speech into conformity with the words heard. But to go amongst native speakers without previous preparation simply means waste of time, and the amount acquired will be very little indeed. The present manual indicates the general lines to be followed, and if the work here outlined is done carefully it ought not to be difficult to pick up a fair speech in a short time.

As for (iii) and (iv), these requirements are best covered by an elementary knowledge of grammar. It is hardly possible for us to learn a foreign language in the same way that a child learns his native speech; for one thing we could not afford to spend the ten or twelve years which a child takes before it learns to speak intelligently, nor could we give the undivided attention which it gives, having a mind as yet unoccupied by any other language. We need some shorter method, and grammar is an attempt to shorten the work by giving general rules and guiding principles which help us to cover the ground more quickly. In a language like Arabic, where so many words are formed on standard "measures", grammar may help us to acquire an extensive vocabulary in a fairly short time. But it must be understood that any "rules" are not the theoretical ideas of pundits, but simple statements intended to save the learner's time and trouble. At the same time it is well to bear in mind that amongst Arabs a knowledge of grammar is the hall-mark of an educated man.

A manual like the present is necessarily written more or less on the supposition that the learner is trying to teach himself. Of course, this is not the ideal method, but it seems most satisfactory that rules should be explained in such simple terms that they do not necessarily require further explanation by a teacher, though such addition may be of assistance. It is probable that, in most cases at least, anyone taking up the subject of Arabic will be an adult, but in spite of this there are certain " rules ", conclusions learned in the course of practical work, which still seem convenient. In the first place even an adult, himself desirous of mastering the language, is deterred by the appearance of difficulty and views jealously the length of the portions set for him to master; this being the case, it is important that the " rules " be stated as briefly as is consistent with clearness and the illustrations be no more than reasonably suffice to make the meaning clear. It does not seem expedient to take for granted even the simpler principles and processes of grammar, which up to a point are common to English and Arabic and then diverge on different lines; it seems safer to state even simple points which are probably known to the average learner rather than to allow anyone to waste time in searching for the meaning. It will probably happen that the learner will sometimes work with a native teacher, and may then experience either a lack of systematic method or the assumption of grammatical principles quite different from those learned in an English education, and his only safeguard will be a plain statement in the very simplest terms of the chief principles underlying the language. The matter in which the average learner most needs help is the way in which words should be grouped together so as to form intelligible sentences, and in this instruction cannot be too simple and detailed.

It may be presumed that anyone who takes up the study of colloquial Arabic intends to make colloquial use of it, and so to mingle in intercourse with Muslims. In such intercourse etiquette means a very great deal, and such etiquette means a rather elaborate and formal politeness which is valued much more than the hearty good-fellowship which is preferred by Westerns. Some of the younger generation are inclined to discard this and to adopt a brusque free and easy tone, which they suppose to be more "European" and so more modern. It is generally best not to encourage this; quite unintentionally it is likely to lead to familiarities which will be distasteful and not at all easy to stop, whilst such familiarities displayed before onlookers will seriously damage their esteem of the one who permits them. It is much better to keep to the formal and conventional usages of established custom, to know and use them stamps one as a civilized person in Arab eyes and is respected even by those who pride themselves on being most modern. A European is narrowly watched, and the treatment he receives will depend largely upon his own attitude. Nearly everyone who speaks of "natives" with strong dislike and finds intercourse with them intolerable will be found guilty of one or more of three defects, either (i) he has never mastered enough of the language to make himself understood or to understand what is said to him, or (ii) he has encouraged familiarities and then resented their natural consequences, or (iii) he has scorned the forms of politeness and consequently has not been treated with respect. Some people, admittedly, are unable to adapt themselves to standards different from those to which they have been accustomed, and some regard differences of manner and colour with aversion; for such there is no alternative but to stay in their own country. A person able and willing to adapt himself to Muslim standards will find much courtesy, a great deal of friendliness, and in spite of what is commonly said will, I believe, meet with some real attachment. But the open display of gratitude and sympathy which is encouraged and esteemed in the West is not expected, desired, or encouraged in the East. After a death the expression of the conventional forms of condolence is greatly esteemed, but the expression of sympathy is not asked for, nor desired ; in most cases it would not be understood. " I have given a dying creature the draught of water that has saved his life, and heard him thank God in accents of the most heartfelt gratitude, without so much as a 'Go to' for me" (Keane, *Six months in the Hejaz*, p. 192). Exactly; thanks always are given to God, not to the person who has conferred the benefit, and this should not be expected. The further we move from cosmopolitan centres such as Alexandria, Cairo, and Beirut, the more punctilious should our manners become, until amongst the desert tribe courtesy takes the most elaborate and conventional form and meets with similar courtesy in return.

Courtesy involves the use of many special phrases to which Muslims attach great importance, but which Englishmen are sometimes tempted to regard as waste of time ; their use gives the impression that the speaker is a man of culture and causes him to be treated with more respect, and others are then more ready to be at his service, which means a saving of time in the long run. Some of the commoner forms will be noted in the following pages as opportunity arises.

Unrestrained laughter rather tends to lower one in the eyes of Arab observers ; one should keep a dignified yet cordial attitude without an air of aloofness. It is customary to permit servants, villagers, etc., a greater familiarity of speech than is usual in modern England, but the forms of respect should be expected and their absence corrected. Conversation is sprinkled with many religious expressions, and religious topics enter more freely than is customary in this country. These expressions should be used in the recognized way, but no discussion or inquiry about religion should be entered upon the Muslim does not welcome outside interest or criticism in such matters, but opens out when he finds that one's attitude is neither hostile nor supercilious; the subject must be started by him. Do not try to purchase a copy of the Qur'an, and if you have one keep it carefully out of sight when a Muslim calls upon you. Be careful not to touch one in a mosque or house. You can usually visit mosques if you take off your boots (sometimes over-shoes are provided so that this is not necessary), but you may not attend the services. Generally one is not permitted to enter a chapel where a saint's body is buried.

Pigs and dogs are unclean. It is best not to include pork or bacon amongst one's provisions, or to wear gloves or gaiters of pig-skin or dog-skin. Do not try to make friends with a dog or to pat his head.

The Qur'an forbids the making of images. The Ulema of the al-Azhar mosque hold that this does not forbid the taking of photographs, but many old-fashioned people of the stricter sort object to photographs, and some of the more ignorant peasants and desert Arabs fear that the one who owns a photograph may perhaps have some power for evil over the one depicted, so do not assume that the taking of photographs will always be welcome. In strictly Muslim countries coins and postage stamps do not bear representations of any human figure and it is prudent for a commercial agent not to show trade catalogues containing pictures of human beings: it is often likely to cause aversion.

In eating and drinking only the right hand should be used, and, of course, it is necessary to shake hands (if this is done) with the right. The left hand is used only for purposes which though necessary are unclean.

It is a grave discourtesy to refer to the women of a family;

no inquiry after them can be made nor any remark which betrays a consciousness of their existence. Never should any remark be made which sounds like admiration of children or a compliment on their good looks, good health, etc., and if by inadvertence any such comment is made or heard it is proper to add "I take refuge with the Lord of the day-break" (cf. p. 147); those are the opening words of a *Sura* in the Qur'an, which continues in words which are taken as an exorcism of the evil eye: neglect of this precaution may cause one to be held responsible if the child is taken ill or suffers any misfortune. In no case admire what belongs to another, it is practically asking for a gift; admire a thing only as that which God has created (cf. p. 147 for a suitable form).

Practise privately the manner of sitting on cushions or on a divan without a chair: you will find chairs are rare outside the large towns. Also take some private practice in eating without the help of spoon or fork. It is best to be a strict abstainer in intercourse with Muslims. The use of wine is unlawful to them, and it is a great relief when they find that you do not expect any to be procured for you. If a Muslim, himself a strict abstainer, sends for spirits or beer for you you are likely to get some abomination decocted by a Greek trader, and your well-intentioned host will wonder why you find it so hard to finish what he took no little trouble to procure. When you find men accustomed to drink spirits you may generally suspect that they are not the most reputable members of the community.

Chapter II

PRONUNCIATION

(1) The Consonant Sounds

The Arabic alphabet contains twenty-seven consonant sounds, which may be represented by :—

', b, t, th, g, *h*, kh, d, dh, r, z, s, sh, *s*, *d*, *t*, *z*, ', gh, f, q, k, l, m, n, h, w, y.

It will be noticed that there is no p or v and the Arab usually cannot pronounce these sounds so the loan words "post" and "police" appear as "busta" and "bulis". Most of the consonants given do not present any great difficulty, and those represented by b, t, d, z, s, f, k, l, m, n, h, w, y, nearly resemble the letters so denoted in English, though with differences of timbre which must be learned by imitation of native speakers.

(a) *The Emphatic Consonants.*

It will be noted that the sounds t, d, s, z, and h are given twice over, once in ordinary type and once in italic. The sounds represented by the italic letters are those which give much trouble to English speakers, and must be mastered carefully. For the first four, *t*, *d*, *s*, *z*, take two words for each, one containing the letter as initial, the other containing it as a final, thus for *t* take the English words top, hot—for *d* take day, had—for *s* take such as sop, boss, and for *z* substitute *z*- for *s*- in the preceding. After pronouncing the word naturally, repeat it several times, each time exaggerating the t, d, etc., sound and dwelling upon it until you feel that you are making yourself ridiculous by the amount of exaggeration; the first time you hear a native speaker you will find that he exaggerates it even more than you have done. But whilst exaggerating these sounds you must also try to thrust them a little further back into the throat. The emphatic or exaggerated *z* is for Syria and Egypt alone: in 'Iraq its sound will be that of the *th* at the beginning of such words as "there, then", much emphasized; this is the truer sound and very often in Egypt *z* is altered to *d*, which is an attempt to reproduce it more truly. You must remember that in all these dialects Arabic is spoken by those whose ancestors learned it as a foreign language, and so have never completely attained ease in the use of sounds which were not in their own former language. The true sound of the emphatic letters can only be heard from the lips of a desert Arab.

The emphatic *h* is a consonant which usually gives much trouble to English learners. You must breathe out over this aspirate with more force than over an ordinary h, and dwell longer on the sound, it is an h with an aspiration produced with effort, but in which no other sound than pure h should enter. Such a word as ya*h*fazak is a fair test of one's ability to speak Arabic intelligibly.

In similar way q is really the emphatic form of k, and here it is possible to perceive the real difference between the simple and emphatic consonants by contrasting the initial sounds in the words "king" and "queen".

(b) *The Dental Aspirates.*

The two sounds given as th and dh occur in English and present no difficulty to an English learner. The sound th is that which appears at the beginning of such words as "thin", "theory", "three", and as final in "with", "truth", etc. The sound dh is the softer th which commences such words as "than", "then", "there". But these sounds, correctly pronounced by the desert Arabs, have always proved difficult to the people of Syria and Egypt, and in a less degree to those of 'Iraq. As a result th is sounded either as t or as s, dh as d or z. In Egypt the sounds are generally t and d, in Syria they are most often t and d but s and z also occur. In the following pages, where we are concerned with colloquial speech, the th and dh will rarely occur save in the words peculiar to 'Iraq, but the history of these sounds will explain the apparent inconsistency of t and d occasionally interchanging with s and z. Sometimes the correct th and dh will be heard from the lips of educated persons. Thus the demonstrative pronoun "this" appears in 'Iraq as hâ-dhâ, in Syria it becomes hâ-dâ, and in Egypt the first syllable is dropped and we have dâ. Both in Syria and Egypt this da can be heard as zâ, and that pronunciation is often regarded as *nahwi* or "grammatical". Wherever there is Turkish or Persian influence there is a strong tendency to use s and z not only for the classical th and dh, but even for the emphatic *t* and *d*, thus a Persian will speak of a qâdî, "judge," as a qâzî: it is well to bear in mind that there is a strong Persian element in 'Iraq, and the Turkish element is still well represented amongst the higher orders in Egypt and Syria.

(c) *The Laryngals.*

The kh sound is often difficult to Englishmen; it is the same as the "ch" in Scottish words, such as "loch", etc., or German "hoch". Three consonants are left which we have represented by the signs ', ', and gh. Make a slight pause and then say such a word as "and"; you will notice that as you commence the vowel sound your throat makes a contraction which is just audible as an effort at the beginning. This effort is the Hamza, which we represent by '. It is quite easy at the beginning of a word but it is not easy to introduce it at the close of a syllable. Natives find it quite as difficult as we do, and it generally results simply in lengthening the vowel which goes before, so that one commonly hears râs for ra's, or else it is changed to w or y, so that we get the classical qara' "read" treated as though it were qaray. A careful observance of the correct sound is the mark of a well educated man or of a desert Arab, who, of course, produces these sounds quite naturally. The sound ' is the same, but made emphatic, so as to seem like a catch in the throat; try the effort with which you begin to say the word "and" after a pause, then increase this effort and exaggerate it as much as you can, at the same time trying to thrust it back into your throat. The gh is best described as an attempt at gargling; if you cannot succeed in this sound make it like a hard g emphasized.

Pains must be taken especially over the emphatic consonants, which in many cases entirely change the meaning of a word. It is ludicrous to hear a missionary telling people that God wants a man's kalb, "dog," when he really means qalb, "heart." So sif means "sword", but *s*if = "summer", sew*t* = "whip", *s*awt = "voice", fikr = "thought", faqr = "poverty", fitna = "sedition", fu*t*na = "prudence", in many cases the short vowel being obscure so that the difference in the vowel sounds is scarcely audible.

Do not be discouraged at the difficulty of some of the sounds. You cannot learn fluent Arabic by yourself, and probably no teacher, however efficient, can make you correct ; all you can do is to get some approximate pronunciation which may be understood by a patient listener, then, when opportunity offers, you must spend your time in the midst of an Arabic-speaking community and by hearing and imitating will soon learn to speak intelligibly. The better your previous knowledge of grammar and vocabulary the quicker will this result be attained.

See below (sect. 4) for notes on some of the chief differences in pronunciation between Egypt, Syria, and 'Iraq.

(2) The Long Vowels and Diphthongs

The vowel sounds properly are three only, a, i, and u. When long these are pronounced thus :—

â as a in " father ", " rather ", etc.

î as the ee in " feet ", " sweet ", etc.

û as the oo in " moon ", " soon ", etc.

Very soon, however, the â inclines towards the a in " fate ", and this is particularly the case in Egypt, but the true ah sound (as above) is always intelligible and preferable.

ê is pronounced like the a in " rate ", " hate ", etc.

ô is like the long o in " holy ", " roll ", etc.

These two long vowels are really diphthongs, ê = ay, ô = aw, and remembering this will greatly help to explain the cases in which they occur, e.g. the verb *t*afayt becomes necessarily *t*afêt, " I extinguished " ; the grammars call this an " irregular " verb, but if we remember the origin of the e there is no irregularity but simply the application of a phonetic rule.

(3) The Short Vowels

The short vowels are a, i, u. Very commonly a can be sounded as e and even as i, provided it does not come next to one of the h, *h*, kh, or ' sounds. This modification of a is most common in Egypt, but such variation will be found in different degrees in local dialects, often differing in districts quite near one another. All the short vowels are obscured by the fact that Arabic is a more "throaty" language than English, the sounds are thrust more back into the throat and the throat muscles exercised more freely than in speaking English. We may regard the short a as an obscured a like that in the English word "beggar". Unless we are trying to reproduce accurately the local dialect of some particular district there is no need to be strictly consistent in the rendering of the short a: we may say al-madîne, el-medîne, or il-medîne. In the following pages the short a generally appears as e unless near one of the consonants which restrain the modification, and this is the most practical representation, though the Egyptian peasant will most often sound it as i. On the other hand, the more educated tend to reproduce the purer a sound. So short i may often sound as e, and short u generally does sound like o. After or before an emphatic consonant (one of those here given in italics) all the short vowels incline towards an o-u sound. But you will find much diversity in the sounding of short vowels, not only between one district and another, but even between different quarters of the same town, and sometimes the difference shows whether the speaker is a Muslim, or a Jew, or a Christian. Unless you desire to make a detailed study of peculiarities of dialect it is hardly necessary to acquire these very accurately. Willmore, in his *Spoken Arabic of Egypt* (p. 10), gives the sensible remark, "take care of the consonants and the vowels will take care of themselves," referring, of course, to the short vowels. He further notes that "Vowels are in English pronounced more in the front of the mouth, in Cairene Arabic more in the upper part of the throat ", and so " vowels are one and all thicker and more rounded in Arabic than they are in our language ". But again it must be repeated that we can at best get only a rough approximation until we actually hear the spoken language and set ourselves to reproduce what is heard, not the speech of one teacher but the natural converse of many who are speaking without any effort to make their words intelligible to a foreigner ; it is only by a stay in an Arabic speaking atmosphere that any satisfactory colloquial powers can be developed.

(4) Word Structure

In Arabic every syllable must be pronounced quite distinctly, and so in qattal it must be clear that there are two t's, as qat-tal, for qatal is a different word not quite the same in meaning. The Arab cannot normally sound a consonant without the help of a vowel, and so " Platon " (Plato) becomes " Aflatun " and " Frank " appears as " Ifrang " or " Firang ", and when three consonants come together it is necessary to insert a vowel, usually -i-, sometimes a vowel assimilated to another near. As modern Arabic has lost the vowel endings which in ancient Arabic marked the cases of nouns and the moods of verbs, it often happens that this addition has to be made. Thus shuft = " I saw " and " I saw her ", ought to be shuftha, but as this would mean three consonants together it becomes shuftiha; but "I saw them" changes shufthum to shuftuhum, where -u- is due to the vowel following. Arabs who are able to sound a consonant group without sufficient vowel help have learned to do so in schools where they have been in contact with European teachers, and their speech is no t to be copied. InWestern speech (i.e. the Arabic of Morocco, Algeria, and Tunis) the tendency is to slur over short unaccented vowels, and so the words seem to contain grouped consonants, but in reality it is that the short vowel is hurried over and has only about half the time value of an ordinary short vowel. Thus in Egypt, etc., we find *s*aba*h* = "morning", but in the West this becomes *s*'ba*h*; the first -a- is like the "obscure" a in "beggar", but reduced to about half its duration. This shortening of the unaccented vowels before the accent is one of the most characteristic marks of "Western" Arabic, and it is well to note that Western influences extend right up to the western suburbs of Alexandria.

Accentuation, i.e. the emphasis due to the accent of stress as on the e in "invent", varies and its variations are amongst the characteristics distinctive of the different dialects. Originally, no doubt, the accent generally rested on the penultimate or syllable before the last, but the decay of the final vowels used to denote cases and moods has caused the tendency to accentuate the last syllable of a word. In the colloquial speech of Syria and Lower Egypt the accent rests on the last syllable when that syllable has a long vowel or a short vowel followed by two consonants; if the last syllable is short and closed by one consonant the accent generally falls on the preceding syllable. The present accentuation of Syria and Lower Egypt, in which the accent is controlled by the vowel quantity, seems to be the Syrian usage which has been adopted by scholars and gradually spread by their influence. The rustic speech of Egypt rather tends to advance the accent towards the end of the stem, and this, probably the older usage, is still further emphasized in Maghrabi, i.e. "Western" Arabic, and largely accounts for the slurring over of a preceding short vowel: thus in Egypt and Syria we hear **ánta,** "thou," but in the West this becomes antá and even nta. (See p. 34 below.) Attention should be paid to differences of accent in speech, as these will often furnish a key to the local dialect, which at first seems so different from Arabic heard elsewhere. In so far as local dialect is distinguished by peculiarity of accent, this will be found to follow some particular tendency fairly consistently, and the tendency will soon be noted by the attentive listener.

(5) Dialectal Differences

(a) *Consonant g.*

In Egypt the g is sounded hard, as in the English word "garden", but elsewhere it is soft, as in "general". This is to be taken as distinctive of the Egyptian dialect. When Syria was given back to Turkey in 1840—it had been attached to Egypt in 1833—some of the Egyptians who had settled there wanted to remain and pretended to be Syrians. The test used was to make them pronounce the word for "camel"; if they said "jemel" they were accepted as Syrians, but if they said "gemel" with a hard g they were sent back to Egypt. In the following pages the letter is always written g, for g is allowed to have both sounds, but note that in Syria and 'Iraq g has to be pronounced soft, like an English j, but in Egypt it has to be a hard g as in "gold". When Greek and other words containing hard g are put into Arabic the letter gh is generally used. Occasionally some peculiar renderings of the g sound may be heard, due to dialectal tendencies amongst those who are least in touch with the outer world. Thus amongst the fellahin and Bedwin of Upper Egypt a "dy" sound can be heard making gemel, "camel" sound like dyamel (diamel), and along the Lower Euphrates this goes further and produces a y sound, making "yemel", etc. On the other hand, the soft g sound (like j or the g in English " gem ") becomes zh (i.e. like the -dg- in " edge ") along the Syrian coast and amongst the Christian population of Jerusalem. As the various religious communities in the East live very much amongst themselves and do not mix with those of other religions, it is not uncommon to find dialectal peculiarities which betray a man's religious adherence.

(b) *Consonant k.*

Usually there is no difficulty about the pronunciation of the consonant k, but in 'Iraq sometimes we find k with vowel -i- sounded as ch, like the initial of the English word " church " contrasted with the Scottish " kirk ". Thus " thy " addressed to a woman is -ik in Egypt, Syria, etc., but -ich (as though -itch) in 'Iraq. This is not exclusive to 'Iraq, however, as it may be heard also amongst the Bedwin of the Syrian desert and the fellahin of Palestine.

(c) *Consonant q.*

The sound represented as q in the following pages is as the q followed by -u- in such English words as "question", "queen", etc. It will be noted that it is thrust further down into the throat than the ordinary k and so tends to affect the vowel sound following; a similar (inevitable) modification of the vowel sound occurs in Arabic, and results from contact not only with q but with all the " emphatic " sounds, i.e. those which are represented by italics in this book. In Upper Egypt, and to some extent also in 'Iraq, and amongst the desert Arabs generally, this q is sounded as g, and so we hear gâl (= qâl), " say ", gult (= qult), " I said ", Gurnah (for Qurnah) as the name of a well-known village near Theves, and this modification of q to g hard should be borne in mind by anyone in Upper Egypt, and should be actually adopted by those who are living in ‘Iraq. It is not, however, usual thus to sound the first letter of the name of the holy book, the Qur’ân. In Lower Egypt, in the towns of Syria, and in the neighbourhood of Jerusalem the q has quite a different sound and becomes either the strong effort we have represented by (‘) or the weaker effort (’), or passes away altogether. Thus the words qâm qâl = “ he began to say ” (lit. “ he arose, he said ”) may be heard as gâm gâl in Upper Egypt and ‘Iraq, as ‘âm ‘âl or even âm âl in Lower Egypt, etc. Occasionally the q sound becomes the strong gh, the gargling sound which is best learned by trying to imitate the grunting sound a camel makes ; this particular modification will be met with in certain districts of ‘Iraq, often amongst the Bedwin. Near Jerusalem q often sounds as k.

(d) *The Aspirate Consonants.*

As we have already noted, the sounds th, dh, are rendered truly in ‘Iraq (as a rule), but generally become t, d, in Egypt and Syria, sometimes s, z, which shows an (unsuccessful) effort to give the true sounds (and so likely to be met with in the partly-educated) or else betrays a Turkish or Persian influence. In some cases, however, the z for dh is fairly regular, e.g. it is quite common in Egypt to hear ki-za = “ thus ”, “ like this ”, for ka-dha.

(e) *The Vowels.*

Both in Egypt and Syria, perhaps to a less extent in ‘Iraq there is a general tendency to weaken short -a- to -e- and -i-, in Lower Egypt the -i- is the commonest resultant, and so we hear ir-râgil, “ the man,” rather than er-râgil, but the -i-, -e- of this sort is the obscure vowel of indistinct timbre, especially the unaccented short before the accent, in “ Western ” Arabic (Morocco, etc.), very often such vowels disappear altogether, and there we hear "m'dîne" for "medîne", etc. In the following pages this short vowel is most often represented by -e-, but we have not kept to this consistently, it is sometimes -a-, sometimes -i-, and it is best for the learner to regard these sounds as fluctuating, not definitely fixed; very often a perceptible variation may be heard within a few miles distance or in adjacent districts in a town. When in contact with a "throat" sound such as ḥ, kh, ', or one of the emphatic letters, the -a- sound should be preserved, and in any passages of "classical" character, e.g. quotations, etc., this should be done. The dictum of the grammarians is that -a- is always correct, -e-, -i- is permitted under certain conditions, and these conditions colloquial speech extends far beyond anything the grammarians approved.

CHAPTER III

THE FIRST LESSON—THE NOUN AND THE SIMPLE NOMINAL SENTENCE

(1) FOR convenience we start with the classification of words according to the grammarians, who divide them into (i) nouns, (ii) verbs, and (iii) particles. Every sentence contains a noun expressed or implied, sentences which contain verbs are called " verbal sentences ", those which do not are called " nominal sentences " ; the particles are used only as accessory to verbs and nouns. The noun or name (ism) is the name of anything which may be real, as " man ", " house ", etc., or merely an idea as " virtue ", " truth ", etc., or may be a quality (adjective) as " black ", " good ", etc., or a pronoun such as " he ", " this ", etc. All these are classed together as nouns and the function which any one of them fulfils in a sentence normally holds good for any other.

Nouns thus include :—

(*a*) Substantives (i) names of real things, (ii) names of ideal things (abstract nouns), including the infinitives of verbs.

(*b*) Adjectives or descriptives, including participles of verbs.

(*c*) Pronouns.

(2) THE DEFINITE AND INDEFINITE

Nouns may be *definite* and so denote one particular person or thing, as " Muhammad ", " Cairo ", " he ", etc.—or they may be *indefinite* and so denote any one of a class, as " man ", " town ", etc. Proper names and pronouns are definite by their own nature. An indefinite noun becomes definite by having the defining article " the " placed before it, as indefinite " man ", definite " the man ".

(3) The Defining Article

In Arabic the defining article " the " is l-. When this is preceded by a vowel the l- alone suffices, as in abû l-walad = " the father of the boy ", where l- does not need anything further to enable it to be pronounced. When it is not preceded by a vowel the sound a- or e- (Egyptian often i-) is added (as already explained e-, i-, are only dialectal modifications of short a- not next to a throat sound), and so " the " = al-, el-, or il-. Thus walad = " boy ", el-walad = " the boy ".

But when the noun following begins with one of the letters t, ṭ, th, d, ḍ, dh, s, ṣ, sh, z, ẓ, r, or n, the l- assimilates to that letter and so " the man " = er-râgil (not el-râgil, though that is written in Arabic but pronounced with the assimilation), so shams = " sun", ash-shams = "the sun", etc. (In Egyptian dialect the same assimilation is sometimes applied to k- and so we hear ak-kull for al-kull = " the whole " ; this is a piece of dialect and should not be regarded as regular. In the following pages the article l-, al-, el-, il-, is written thus with the hyphen connecting it with the noun it defines.

(4) The Indefinite

There is no Arabic word for the indefinite " a " or " an ". If we mean " a man " we say simply râgil = " man " without adding any article ; if we mean " a certain man " we may use the numeral wâhid = " one " and say " one man ", or we may express " a certain town " by a paraphrase " a town from the towns ", e.g. fi medîna min medayîn eṣ-Ṣîn = " in a certain town of China " (= in a town of the towns of China. Story of 'Ala d-Din).

The word wâḥid is the numeral " one ", and is used with the masculine as wâhid walad = " a certain boy ", with the feminine it is waḥde as waḥde bint = " a certain girl ". It naturally cannot be used in the plural and there its nearest equivalent is ba'ḍ " some " (cf. p. 85 below).

Very often Arabic requires the definite article where it is not required in English, e.g. with abstract nouns as el-'adl = "justice", and such as eṣ-ṣêf, " summer," in fi ṣ-ṣêf = " in summer " ; sometimes it may be used or omitted without difference to the meaning, as el-arba'a nuṣṣ et-tamanya *or* arba'a nuṣṣ tamanya = " four is half of eight ".

(5) The Descriptive

The adjective or other descriptive (noun in apposition, participle) follows the noun it describes, thus râgil = " man ", kebîr = " great ", râgil kebîr = " great man ", Muhammad esh-shêkh = " Muhammad the sheikh," etc.

If the first noun is defined the descriptive which follows must also be defined, if the first is indefinite the descriptive must be undefined also, thus râgil kebîr = " great man ", er-râgil el-kebîr = " the great man ", Muḥammad el-kebîr = " the great Muhammad ", where the proper name is defined by its own nature.

Proper names are necessarily definite, but there are some which originally were common nouns and have become proper names ; these may have the article, but they may equally well appear without, the addition or omission of the article makes no difference ; thus we may say Ḥasan or el-Ḥasan, both are equally correct, and both are equally defined.

If the noun defined be feminine the descriptive adjective must be feminine also, the feminine being usually formed by adding -a* or -e* to the masculine, thus kebîr = "great" (of a man), kebîre = "great" (of a woman). Thus final -a, -e, represents an ancient -at, -et, of which the -t has fallen away. In Hebrew, which may be regarded as an early dialect of colloquial Arabic, the change had already taken place in the Siloam inscription written under the old Hebrew monarchy—but when the termination is not a final, i.e. when a suffix is added or a genitive is attached, the -t is preserved, so medîne appears as medînet, kebîre as kebîret, etc. In the vocabularies below we mark this termination *, e.g. medîne*, etc.

Normally the male is masculine, the female is feminine, but care must be taken not to assume that the genders of grammar necessarily connect with the sexes: things without life, and so without sex, are still treated as masculine or feminine. Usually words ending in -a, -e, are feminine, as medîne, "city," but the feminine form of the adjective is regularly used with the (collective) plural (see p. 68 below), and very generally the -a*, -e*, ending is added to denote the individual of a species, e.g. naml = "ants", namle* = "a single ant", etc., so we must not assume that grammatical gender (whatever its origin) is always connected with sex, nor are we entitled to assume that the Arabs because they make all nouns masculine or feminine therefore regarded every object in nature as alive, an unverified idea which has become popular with some theorists.

(6) The Simple Nominal Statement

We see that râgil kebîr = "great man", and er-râgil el-kebîr = "the great man", in either case the adjective agrees with the preceding noun in being defined or undefined. If we say—

er-râgil kebîr

we get a simple nominal statement meaning "the man is great". There is no need to translate the word "is" into Arabic, the sentence is complete as it stands, and on this model a large number of simple, but very useful, sentences can be formed. The simple form we thus use as a model contains two elements, (i) a defined noun referring to some person or thing already known to us, and (ii) a new piece of information now first added to our previous knowledge. Thus :—

er-râgil marîḍ	= *The man is ill*
er-râgil el-kebîr marîḍ	= *The great man is ill*
Muḥammad esh-shêkh el-kebîr marîḍ	= *The great shêikh Muhammad is ill.*

We shall see later that as the sentence becomes longer it becomes more usual to "resume" the thread of our speech by inserting a pronoun, as "the great sheikh Muhammad (he) is ill", etc., but we still have a perfectly sound model in our general scheme of :—

(i) A noun defined and already known ;

(ii) An additional piece of information conveyed by a noun undefined.

Sentences of this "nominal" time are only descriptive; they cannot be used to describe events taking place in time. Thus I can say "Muhammad is great" in two words, (i) the defined name (defined by its own nature), and (ii) the undefined information now added ; but if I mean "Muhammad is great" in the sense that he is so now but was formerly not so, i.e. "he has become great", or if I mean "he is great" in the sense that he now is but will cease to be so, in either of these cases I must use a verb meaning "be, is", etc. A sentence without a verb can be only descriptive without reference to a happening in time.

(7) The Interrogative Sentence

Any sort of statement in Arabic can be turned into a question in any one of three ways, (i) it may be spoken in an interrogative tone of voice, and this rising tone is denoted in the following pages by the use of the sign (?): thus er-râgil kebîr = "the man (is) great," er-râgil kebîr ? = "is the man great?"—interrogative simply by reason of the tone in which it is uttered. (ii) Or the particle hal, or the prefix 'a- may be used before the sentence; this is the classical usage and is now rare save in the speech of the educated. Or (iii) an interrogative pronoun or compound derived from a pronoun may be used, as el-medine fên ? = "the town (is) where ?" (i.e. "where is the town ?").

A fourth way (iv) may be mentioned as heard in vernacular (or vulgar) speech, which adds -sh, or -esh, meaning shay = "thing, somewhat," etc., to the word which is the subject of question, e.g. 'etshân = "thirsty," 'etshânesh ? = "at all thirsty ?" i.e. "are you at all thirsty ?"

(8) General Summary of this Lesson

(*a*) Nouns are *defined* (made to refer to a particular individual) (i) by their own nature (proper names, pronouns, etc.); (ii) by the prefixed article.

(*b*) Article "the" = l-, al-, el-, il-. l- assimilates before t, ṭ, th, d, ḍ, dh, s, ṣ, sh, z, ẓ, r, n.

(*c*) Order: substantive—adjective (or descriptive noun), both of same gender, equally defined or undefined.

(*d*) Nominal sentence: (i) Subject of which statement is

made—defined. (ii) Predicate, the statement made about it—undefined.

(*e*) Interrogative: Made so (i) by tone of voice, (ii) by particle hal, or prefixed a-, (iii) by interrogative pronoun, (iv) by added -sh, -esh.

VOCABULARY I

(i) *Adjectives of the measure qaîl.*

It will greatly ease our labour in learning vocabularies of Arabic words if we note that many words are formed on regular "measures". Thus we note that adjectives such as kebîr "great", ketîr "much", ṣaghîr "little", etc., are formed on the measure -a-î-, or -e-î- (where -e- is, of course, a dialectal variation of -a-), that is to say, each contains three consonants with -a- or -e- between the first and second, long -î- between the second and third. All these form their feminine by adding -a or -e which becomes -at, -et, before a suffix or connected word. In the vocabulary adjectives of this kind are fairly numerous. For the present we will content ourselves with twelve specimens of such adjectives:—

faqîr	= *poor*	neḍîf	= *clean*
gedîd	= *new*	qelîl	= *little, small (quantity)*
kebîr	= *great*	qaṣîr	= *narrow, short*
ketîr	= *much*	qawî	= *strong*
leṭîf	= *pretty*	ṣaghîr	= *small (in size)*
marîḍ	= *ill*	ṭawîl	= *long*

All these are of the same "measure" *qatîl*, though one (qawi) does not at first seem to fit in. This introduces us to what is called an "irregular" form, though, in fact, the majority of such irregularities in Arabic are simply instances of phonetic modifications which are all subject to certain fixed principles.

This word, for example, is properly qawîy and might be so written, but it is impossible to give a separate consonant sound to -y after -i in any language unless another vowel follows, then it can be sounded clearly, and thus the feminine is qawîyye*. In Lower Egypt the words qelîl, qawi, will sound as 'elîl, 'awi (see p. 19 above), and in 'Iraq qawi sounds gawi, guwi, with hard g- (see p. 18 above). These differences occur whenever a word contains q, and we shall not return to them again in each case, but content ourselves with noting the general dialectal tendency.

(ii) *Strengthening of the Adjective.*

The adjectives ketîr, qawi, as well as the adjective giddan = "very" can be added to other adjectives as a means of strengthening, thus leṭîf = "pretty", leṭîf qawi = "very pretty", leṭîf qawi ketîr = "very very pretty", "very pretty indeed", also halqêt (peculiar to Palestine). Adverbs properly do not occur in Arabic, they are nouns (or adjectives) used adverbially and (originally) with the accusative -an added, so that the classical forms would be ketîr-an, qawîy(y)-an, gidd-an.

Sometimes we are told that bi-ziyâde = "by excess" serves for the English "too", or the adjective zâyid= "excessive" is thus used, and bi-l-kifâye = "by the sufficiency" for "enough", as kabîr bi-ziyâde, "too large," kab'r bi-l-kifâye, "large enough," and huwa *t*uluh zâyid, "it, its length (is) excessive," but these forms, though they would be understood by an Arab, would never be used by him, they are essentially alien to the spirit and character of Arabic, and we must reconcile ourselves to the fact that "too" and "... enough" cannot be expressed in Arabic. Our only way of saying "too large" is "very, very large" (see Van Ess, *Spoken Arabic of Mesopotamia*, p. 108).

(iii) Particular note must be made of the measure qutayil (for qutayl), which is a diminutive form, and is very much used in colloquial Egyptian and by the Arabs living along the rivers in Mesopotamia. Some of the commonest instances are :—

ṣughayir for ṣaghîr = *little*
kuwayis = *good, pretty*
ṭayyib (for ṭuyayib) = *good*

(iv) *Interrogatives.*

The following list gives the commonest forms of interrogative particles and pronouns :—

ên, wên ('Iraq, Syr.), fên = *Where?*

To this we can add prepositions, and say :—

min ên ? (min wên ?) = *from where? (whence?)*
ila ên ? (ila wên ?) = *to where (whither?)*
kêf, kîf (Syr.) = *how?*
mîn,men ('Iraq) = *who? whom? whose?*

may be used of singular or plural.

mâ (only of things) = *what ?*

in colloquial only used in a few expressions, such as :—

mâ lu ? = *what is the matter with him ?* (lit. *what to him ?*)
ana mâ li ? = *what is that to me ?*
êh, êy, ê = *what ?* singular or plural, the more usual form in colloquial speech.

May have the prepositions added :—

'êh ? (= li-êh) = *for what?—why?*
bi-sabab êy ? = *for what reason?*

'ala shân êy ? ('ashân êy ?) = *why?* (Egyptian)
shû (Syr.), shinû ('Iraq), êsh (Egypt.) = *what?* all these are compounds of shayy = *thing* (cf. Egyptian 'ala shân êy ? above)

(v) *Other particles in common use.*

aiwa (Eg.), na'am (Eg., Syr., 'Iraq), belli ('Iraq only) = *yes*
lâ = *no.* In classical Arabic, sometimes in the speech of those who affect the literary style, and in the dialects of South Arabia this can be used for the ordinary negative *not*
aho, ahe (Egyptian, chiefly) = *here is* (really a demonstrative made from a- (ha-) with the personal pronoun suffixed, see p. 40 below)

(vi) *Nouns Substantive.*

bâb = *door*
bêt = *house* (household, house in town, etc.)
dâr (fem.) = *house* (word used by the Bedwin people of Upper Egypt, etc.)
bint (fem.) = *girl.*
môya (mâ) = *water*
râgil (râgul) = *man*
tarîq (masc. or fem.) = *road, way.*

EXERCISE

(1) bêt kebîr—el-bêt el-kebîr—el-bêt kebîr	= **A large house—the large house—the house is large.**
(2) dâr ṣaghîre—ed-dâr eṣ-ṣaghîre—ed-dâr ṣaghîre	= **A little house—the little house—the house is small.**
(3) eṭ-ṭarîq ṭawîl ?—aiwa, eṭ-ṭarîq ṭawîl ketîr qawi	= **Is the road long?—Yes, the road is very long indeed.**
(4) fên el-bâb ?—ahe el-bâb	= **Where is the door?—Here is the door.**
(5) fên môya ?—aho môya ketîr	= **Where is there water?—Here is plenty of water.**
(6) el-bêt ṭayyib ?—aiwa, el-bêt ṭayyib qawi	= **Is the house all right?—Yes, the house is quite all right.**
(7) el-bint kebîre ?—la, el-bint ṣaghîre (ṣughayire)	= **Is the girl big (old)?—No, the girl is a little one.**
(8) ed-dâr ṭayyibe ?—aiwa, ed-dâr kuwaise kuwaise	= **Is the house nice?—Yes, the house is very nice indeed.**
(9) el-môya ketîr ?—la, el-môya qelîl giddam	= **Is there much water?—No, the water is very scanty,**
(10) er-râgil faqîr qawi	= **The man is very poor.**
(11) fên el-môya ?—aho el-môya	= **Where is the water?—Here is the water.**
(12) el-bêt fên ?—ahe el-bêt	= **Where is the house?—Here it is.**
(13) ed-dâr eṣ-ṣaghîre fên ?	= **Where is the little house?**

Notes

In the words given above long vowels within a word are marked, but final long vowels are not. It may be taken as a general rule that short final vowels have been lost and those represented are, as they stand, long; indeed it is not so easy to pronounce a final short, which is probably the reason why they have dropped out. When suffixes are added, the long, now no longer final, may be shortened or it may remain long, and in this latter case this long vowel is noted like every other long occurring within a word.

It is probably needless to say that it is not practicable to translate literally from one language to another and it is certainly not desirable to make the attempt. In translating from English to Arabic, or from any language to another, the first thing is to observe the meaning at the bottom of the sentence, the next is to express it naturally in the language into which we are making the translation: to translate word for word means certain disaster, we ought not to try to reproduce what we say in the language of the Arab, but rather to express in Arabic the meaning previously expressed in English. For example, if we want to say in Arabic "Is there much water?" the sentence contains four words, but we can dispense with two of these, one "there" thus used is a peculiar English idiom, another "is" is not necessary in an Arabic nominal sentence; it is quite sufficient to say "the water—much?" in an "interrogative" tone of voice, i.e. rising inflection, and we have all that is necessary for an Arabic sentence; the essential points are (1) that we define the "water" as already known to us, and (2) do not define the "much" as being that about which we need information.

Supplementary Note on the Interrogative Pronouns

who?—Classical Arabic man—'Iraq men. mî? Central Arabia, Egypt, Syria, mîn.

what?—(1) mâ (as class. Ar.) rare. m'hu, mu, Oman, 'Iraq.

(2) ayy (class.) êy, ê, (êh), Egypt. êy, ê, eiya, Syria, Palestine, C. Arabia. (With interrogative -sh), êsh, shê, sh, 'Iraq. êsh (Damascus), S. Arabia, Egypt. âsh, Morocco. wush, Transjordania. shû, Syria (= ash-hu).

(3) en-hû, -hî, hum (Egypt). ên-û, -â, -hom, Syria.

which ?—class. Ar. annâ(y), anî, Egypt. anu, anû, Palestine.

Chapter IV

THE SECOND LESSON—THE PERSONAL PRONOUNS AND THE NEGATIVE SENTENCE

(9) We have already used two kinds of nouns, the substantive and the adjective, we now turn to the third kind, the pronoun. The commonest pronoun is the personal " I ", " he ", " she ", etc., and because of its very common use there are perceptible differences in the several dialects, though these are for the most part no more than phonetic modifications.

The personal pronoun appears in two forms, (*a*) the separate form which is used in the nominative " I ", " he ", etc., and (*b*) the suffixed form which is used for the possessive " my ", " his ", etc., or for the objective " me ", " him ", etc. The first form stands alone, the second can only be used attached to a noun, verb, or certain particles.

(10) The Personal Pronoun: Separate Form

Sing. 1. " I " ana, ani.
2. masc. " thou " ente (Eg.), ent (Syr.), inte (Eg., 'Ir.).
fem. " thou " intî (Eg., Ir.), enti (Eg., Syr.).
3. masc. " he " hûwa (Eg., Syr.), hû (Syr.), hû'a ('Ir.), hûa ('Ir.).
fem. " she " hîya (Eg., Syr.), hî (Syr.), hî'a ('Ir.), hîe ('Ir.).

Plur. 1. " we " eḥna (Eg., 'Ir.), iḥna (Eg., Syr.), neḥn (Syr.).
2. " you " entû (Eg., Syr.), entum (Eg.), intû ('Ir.), intum ('Ir.).
3. " they " hum (Eg., Syr.), humma (Eg., Syr., 'Ir.).

The plural " we " is very often used for the singular " I ", and the plural " you " is used for " thou " though this is not at all so common as in the European languages, and the 2nd person singular is neither familiar nor discourteous. In the compounds ḥaḍretek = " your honour ", etc., it is the most respectful form.

The 3rd person may be used very much as a demonstrative, as in huwa mush ṣâliḥ . . . = " is it not true that . . ."

It is generally possible to omit the personal pronoun when it is obvious, thus 'aṭshânsh ? = " thirsty ? ", i.e. " are you thirsty ? "

The personal pronouns are all defined by their own nature as they refer to known persons or things : thus we form sentences :—

ana faqîr = *I am poor*
ente keslân = *Thou art lazy*
hûwa kebîr qawi = *He is a very great one*, etc.

Very often a personal pronoun is added to a word already defined, and this added pronoun may become necessary when the predicate is also defined. Thus used the pronoun seems to be an equivalent to the verb " to be ", thus—

el-walad hûwa keslân = *The boy* (*he*) *is lazy*
ana hûwa et-tâgir = *I am the merchant*
(*I am he who is the merchant*)
ente hûwa er-râgil ? = *Art thou the man ?*
ente marîḍ ? = *Are you ill ?*
hîya marîḍe = *She is ill*

(11) THE NEGATIVE SENTENCE

A sentence may be made negative by inserting ma ('Iraq mû) before the part denied, as er-râgil ma kebîr = " the man is not great ", but colloquial speech, especially in Egypt and Syria, commonly adds -sh (-she before a following consonant), a corruption of shayy = " thing ", after the word negatived, thus ma anîsh râyiḥ = " I am not going ", tegi = " come ", ma tegish = " do not come ", etc.

Combined with the personal pronouns we get negatives :—

manîsh (ma anîsh)	= *I am not*
mantâsh (ma enta-sh)	= *Thou art not*
mantîsh (ma enti-sh)	= *Thou* (fem.) *art not*
mush (ma hu-sh)	= *He is not*
ma hîsh	= *She is not*
maḥnâsh (ma eḥna-sh)	= *We are not*
mantûsh (ma entû-sh)	= *You are not*
ma humsh	= *They are not*

The 3rd sing. masc. mush is in very general use as a negative particle and may be found with the other persons, thus mush kebîr = " not great ", ana mush gu'ân = " I am not hungry " (vulg.).

Summary of Lesson II

I. Personal pronouns as separate words ana = " I ", ente = " thou ", etc., are used as nominatives.

By nature they are defined as referring to known persons, etc.

In sentences they acquire the meaning of " is ", " are ", etc.

II. Negative Sentences.

Necessary to use ma (mû) = " not ".

Colloquial commonly adds -sh (-she).

lâ = " no " (used for " not " in classical Arabic and in South Arabia).

VOCABULARY TO LESSON II

(i) **Conjunctions.** we- (wa-, wi-) " and " (must be attached to following word). lâkin, we-lâkin " but ".

(ii) Adjectives with -ân, *fem.* -âne*, added to the stem.

‘aṭshân = *thirsty*
gû‘ân = *hungry*
keslân = *lazy, idle*
ta‘bân = *tired*
za‘lân = *angry*

(iii) Other words.

‘êsh = *bread* (Egypt), *life* (elsewhere).
ḥabl = *rope*
hawa = *weather, air*
ḥimâr = *ass*
ḥiṣân = *horse*
khubz = *bread* (Syria, ‘Iraq)
kitâb = *book*
mâl = *property*
mara* = *woman*
ṣa‘ab (ṣa‘b) = *difficult*
shughl = *task, business, work*
tâgir = *merchant*
walad = *child*
kemân = *likewise, also, similarly*

EXERCISE

(For Forms of Address, see p. 39 below).

(1) ente walad keslân = **You are an idle boy.**
(2) la, ya sîdi, manîsh keslân = **No, sir, I am not idle.**
(3) el-bint hîya marîde ?—la, ya sitt, hiya ma hish maride = **Is the girl ill ?—No, madam, the girl is not ill.**
(4) ana faqîr = **I am poor.**
(5) huwa ta‘bân qawi = **He is very tired.**
(6) ya bint, enti keslâne ketîr = **Girl, you are very idle.**
(7) ente ‘aṭshânsh ?—la, ana gû‘ân = **Are you thirsty ?—No, I am hungry.**
(8) el-ḥabl mush ṭawîl ?—aiwa, el-ḥabl ṭawîl ketîr = **The rope is not long (enough) ?—Yes, it is very long (= it is long enough).**
(9) el-mara hiye faqîre = **The woman is poor.**
(10) ana ta‘bân we-gû‘ân = **I am tired and hungry.**
(11) huwa za‘lân ketîr qawi = **He was very angry indeed.**

(12) ed-dâr ma hîsh neḍîfe = **The house is not clean.**

(13) el-walad eṣ-ṣaghîr huwa keslân qawi = **The little boy is very lazy.**

(14) el-mara hîye ta'bâne ketîr = **The woman is very tired.**

(15) el-walad eṣ-ṣaghîr ta'bânsh ? = **Is the little boy tired?**

(16) el-'êsh (khubz) ṭayyib ?—la, el-'êsh mush ṭayyib = **Is the bread good?—No, the bread is not good.**

(17) el-mara el-faqîre hîye ta'bâne ? = **Is the poor woman tired?**

(18) la, we-lâkin hîye gû'âne ketîr = **No, but she is very hungry.**

(19) er-râgil hûwa za'lân qawi = **The man is very angry.**

(20) 'aṭshânsh ?—la, we-lâkin ana gû'ân qawi = **(You) thirsty?—No, but I am very hungry.**

(21) esh-shughli huwa ṣa'ab ketîr = **The work is very hard.**

(Here, as often, it becomes necessary to insert a vowel to prevent three consonants coming in contact. Usually the inserted vowel is -i- or -e-, but it often becomes -u- when the vowel -u- follows in the next syllable. Thus "shughl huwa . . ." has three consonants in contact (of course -gh- is only one consonant sound, though we are obliged to represent it by two letters) and so -i- is inserted between -l and h-, but this must be a very short vowel sound hurried through as much as possible. The necessity of these inserted vowels is increased in the modern colloquial by the loss of the final short vowels used in classical Arabic to denote the cases of nouns and moods of verbs.)

(22) la, esh-shughli mush ṣa'ab ketîr = **No, the work is not very hard.**

(23) gû'ânsh ?—aiwa, we-ana 'aṭshân kemân = **(You) hungry?—Yes, and I am thirsty as well.**

(24) el-mâl ketîr ?—la, el-mâl mush ketîr = **Is the property much?—No, the property is not much.**

(25) er-râgil el-faqîr hûwa gû'ân we-ta'bân kemân = **The poor man is hungry and tired as well.**

(26) el-ḥimâr hûwa keslân qawi—la, mush keslân	= **The donkey is very lazy. No, it is not lazy.**
(27) el-ḥiṣân el-kebîr hûwa ta'bân qawi	= **The big horse is very tired.**
(28) el-bint eṣ-ṣaghîre fên ?—ya sîdi, ahe el-bint eṣ-ṣaghîre	= **Where is the little girl ?—Here is the little girl, sir.**
(29) er-râgil hûwa tâgir we-huwa mush faqîr	= **The man is a merchant and he is not poor.**
(30) el-mara el-faqîre hîya ta'bâne ketîr we-l-bint hiya ta'bâne kemân	= **The poor woman is very tired and the girl is tired as well.**
(31) ente keslânsh ?—la, manîsh keslân	= **Are you lazy ?—No, I am not lazy.**

APPENDIX TO LESSON II

Terms used in Address, etc.

yâ	= *O, call to one near*
ayy-	= *call to one distant*
walad	= *boy*
ṣabiyy	= *boy*
shâbb	= *boy* (courteous form)
ghulâm	= *boy* (only to servant, boy of the lower order, etc.)
kebîr	= *old man* (courteous)
'agûz	= *old woman*
	(In Egypt 'agûz = *old man*, 'agûze = *old woman*)
'ammî	= *my uncle* (polite to elderly man)
shêkh	= *sir* (to elderly man, courteous)
ente	= *you* (to person unknown, familiar)
sayyid	= *sir* (to those who claim to be of the kindred of the Prophet)
sîdî	= *sir* (used by servants, etc., addressing their master)
khawâga	= *sir, Mr.* (middle classes, etc., much used "up country" to Europeans)
effendî (Turkish)	= *sir, Mr.* (officials, clerks, professional classes, etc.)
sitt, sittî	= *madam*
sayyide	= *madam* (to lady of rank)
khâtûn	= (in speaking of, not to, a young lady of good position, in addressing letters, etc.)
ḥaḥratek	= *your honour* (proper form of courteous address)
genâbek	= *your honour* (chiefly to clergy, Europeans, etc.)

Chapter V

THE THIRD LESSON—THE PERSONAL PRONOUN AS SUFFIXES

(12) The personal pronouns ana, ente, etc., which we have already considered, are only used in the nominative, i.e. as meaning "I", "he", "she", etc.; for the oblique cases, possessive such as "my", "his", "our", etc., or objective such as "me", "him", "us", etc., a different system is employed and the pronoun is expressed by a shortened form which is added to the end of a noun, verb, or certain particles. Thus -i is used for "my", e.g. bêti = "my house", ḥiṣâni = "my horse", etc. The suffixes thus used are:—

Sing.	1.	-i	
	2.	masc.	-ak, -ek, -k*
		fem.	ik, -ki*
	3.	masc.	-uh, -u, -o, -h*
		fem.	-ha
Plur.	1.	-na, -ne	
	2.	-kû, -kum, -kon	
	3.	-hum, -um, -om	

The forms marked (*) are only used after vowel endings. For the most part these endings hardly differ in the various dialects, but perhaps 2nd plur. -kû is more often heard in Egypt than elsewhere. The tendency of Syrian Arabic is towards the -o sound for the 3rd masc. sing. and very often the 2nd and 3rd plural in Syria sound -kon, hon. 'Iraq has a peculiar form (sometimes) heard in the 2nd fem. sing.: after a consonant instead of -ik we may get ech, the -ch sounding like the first two letters of "church", which is a palatalized rendering of "kirk". In 'Iraq also we may get -eki, for this person, and -ekum, -ehum in the 2nd and 3rd plur. after a consonant.

Thus bêti = " my house ", bêtek = " thy house ", bêtuh = " his house ", bêtna = " our house ", etc.

A pronominal suffix added to a noun defines it completely just as the article would do, for " my house " specifies a particular house as much as " the house ". Hence we are able to form sentences :—

shughli ṣa'ab	= *My work is difficult*
bêtek wasî'	= *Your house is spacious*
dâruh hîya ṣaghîre	= *His house is small*
bêtna mush kebîr	= *Our house is not large*
hûwa tâgir	= *He is a merchant*
hûwa shughli	= *It is my business*
hîya dârek	= *It is thy house*
bêtkum fên ?	= *Where is your house ?*

When an adjective is added to a word having a suffixed pronoun it is necessary to make the adjective definite to agree with the noun and for this purpose the defining article has to be used :—

bêti el-kebîr	= *My large house*
dâruh eṣ-ṣaghîre	= *His little cottage*

(13) The Suffixes with a Feminine Noun

Feminine nouns in -a*, -e*, as already noted, make this termination into -at, -et, before a suffix, or rather the original -t is preserved by the protection of the suffix. So, medîne " city ", medineti = " my city ", medinetek = " thy city ", medinetha = " her city ", etc.

(14) The Three Nouns of Kinship

The three nouns, ab = " father ", akh = " brother ", and ḥam = " father-in-law ", are treated as though they ended in -û and so make abûk = " thy father ", abûna = " our father ", abûh = " his father ", akhûk = " thy brother ", etc. In the 1st pers. sing. we (usually) find -ye, -ya, -yi added, thus abûya = " my father ", akhûye = " my brother " (also akhui). The " Western " dialect (Morocco, Algiers, etc.) has bûya = " my father ".

abûk hûwa za'lân ? = *Is your father angry ?*
akhûkum eṣ-ṣaghîr hûwa ta'bân qawi = *Your little brother is very tired*
ḥamûha mush ghani = *Her father-in-law is not rich*

(15) Colloquial Insertion of " Property "

Colloquial speech frequently introduces an entirely superfluous noun denoting " property " with the suffixed pronoun after the noun to which the possessive refers, it then becoming necessary that that noun be defined by the addition of the defining article, thus in Egypt we find betâ' (*fem.* betâ't, *plur.* butû') as—

el-kitâb betâ'i = kitâbi = *My book*
ed-dâr betâ'tek = dârek = *Thy house*, etc.

In Syria the inserted word appears as tabâ', *fem.* tabâ't, which is employed in the same way ; and in 'Iraq the word is mâl, as—

al-ḥimâr mâli = ḥimâri = *My ass*

Sometimes also ḥaqq is thus used, chiefly by Bedwin and by tribes bordering on Arabia, as el-kitâb ḥaqqi = kitâbi = " my book ".

The form betâ' is used in Egypt and Palestine, but in Palestine it often becomes taba', presumably a " Spoonerism ". Its original form was metâ', and in Tripoli this is still used and may occur anywhere up to Mex on the western outskirts of Alexandria. In Morocco this contracts to n'tâ' (= netâ' with a very short -e-, note that the -ṭ- has become emphatic) and to ṭâ‘, e.g. l'm'dîna ṭâ‘at s-sulṭân = " the Sultan's city ", which gives a fair idea of the way in which the vowels are " swallowed " in the west, one of the chief difficulties in adapting colloquial Arabic to Western use. In the vernacular of Malta (which is Arabic with a large intrusion of Italian in the vocabulary not in the grammar) this produces the possessive ta = " of ".

In Palestine and Syria we also get shêt, *pl.* shiyût, which appears in the vernacular of Damascus as shît, both derived from shayy(et) " thing ". The form mâl is common in ‘Iraq, spreading down south into Oman and north into Mesopotamia as far at least as Mosul ; ḥaqq or ḥagg properly belongs to South Arabia and is likely to be met with in the speech of seamen from Aden and the district east of that port, practically the only area from which Arab seamen come in any numbers

WORD LIST

(i) Adjectives in ' -i ' making feminine ' -iyye* '.

‘âli	= *high*
ghâli	= *dear* (*in price*)
ghani	= *rich*
radi	= *bad*

(For ' gentile ' nouns in ' -i ' see p. 46 below)

(ii)

ab, abū-	= *father*
akh, akhû-	= *brother*
beled	= *country, town, district*
ḥaiy	= *alive*
ḥâl	= *condition*
ism	= *name* [1]
libâs	= *garment, clothes*
lissa	= *not yet, no longer*
medîne*	= *city*
mubârak	= *blessed* [2]
nehâr	= *day* (*not night*)
rigl	= *foot*
sa‘îd	= *prosperous*
ṣâḥib	= *friend, master*
ṣâliḥ	= *honest*
ṣandûq	= *box*
ukht	= *sister*
umm	= *mother*
wâsi‘	= *broad, spacious*
yôm	= *day* (*twenty-four hours*)

[1] Classical Arabic does not treat the ' i- ' as part of the stem but simply as a prefixed vowel which is dropped after a preceding vowel, but the colloquial treats it as though ' 'ism '.

[2] It is common to hear words beginning in ' mu- ' pronounced as though beginning ' em- '.

EXERCISE

(1) shughlukum ṣa'ab ketîr ? —aiwa, huwa ṣa'ab	= **Is your work very hard?—Yes, it is hard.**
(2) al-walad eṣ-ṣaghîr ismuh êy ?—ya sîdi, ismuh Maḥmûd	= **What is the little boy's name?—Sir, his name is Mahmud.**
(3) er-râgil el-faqîr bêtuh fên ?	= **The poor man, where is his house?**
(4) fên kitâbek ? —ya khawage, ahe el-kitâb betâ'i	= **Where is your book?—Sir, here is my book.**
(5) er-râgil hûwa abûya we-l-walad hûya akhûya ṣ-ṣaghîr	= **The man is my father and the boy is my little brother.**
(6) ahe ummi we-ukhti kemân	= **Here is my mother and my sister as well.**
(7) et-tâgir hûwa ghani we-mâluh ketîr qawi	= **The merchant is wealthy and his property is very great indeed.**
(8) el-'êsh (khubz) ghali giddan	= **The bread is very dear.**
(9) êsh ḥâlek, ya ṣâḥibi ?	= **How are you, my friend?**
(10) ḥimârek (el-ḥimâr betâ'ik) hûwa qawi giddan, we-ḥimâri (el-ḥimâr betâ'i) huwa qawi kemân	= **Your ass is very sturdy and my ass is sturdy also.**
(11) bêtek fên ?	= **Where is your house?**
(12) shughli huwa ṣa'ab ketîr we-ana ta'bân qawi	= **My work is very hard and I am very tired.**
(13) bêto ṣaghîr	= **His house is small.**
(14) bêto eṣ-ṣaghîr mush neḍîf	= **His little house is not clean.**
(15) eṣ-ṣandûq mâlek wên ?—eṣ-ṣandûq mâli hêna (ahe aṣ-sandûq betâ'i)	= **Where is your box?—My box is here.**

(16) dârhum hîye ṣaghîre we-lâkin dâri wâsi'e ketîr	= **Their house is small but my house is very spacious.**
(17) mîn hûwa ?—hûwa abûna	= **Who is he?—He is our father.**
(18) abûkum ismuh êy ?—ismuh Aḥmed we-ismi Aḥmed kemân	= **Your father, what is his name? — His name is Ahmed, and my name is Ahmed as well.**
(19) we-akhûk eṣ-ṣaghîr êsh ismuh ?—ismuh Muḥammad	= **And your little brother, what is his name?—His name is Muhammed.**
(20) abûh tâgir ghani ketîr qawi	= **His father is a very rich merchant.**
(21) et-tâgir el-ghanî mush ṣâliḥ	= **The wealthy merchant is not trustworthy.**
(22) abûkum hûwa ḥaiy ?—la, ya sîdi abûna lissa ḥaiy	= **Is your father alive?—No, sir, our father is no longer alive.**
(23) libâsi el-gedîd hûwa kuwayyis mush ketîr	= **My new clothes are not altogether good.**
(24) ente huwa Muḥammed we-ismuh akhûk ?	= **You who are called Muhammed, what is your brother's name?**

ADDITIONAL EXAMPLES

nehârkum sa'îd = *May your day be prosperous* (= Good day)

(Reply) nehârkum sa'îd we-mubârak = *May your day be prosperous and blessed*

kêf ḥâlkum ?
êsh ḥâlek ? (Syrian) } *How are you?*

(When inquiring after anyone's health the inquirer should gaze earnestly into the face of the one he addresses as though searching for any sign of ill-health. To neglect this makes the inquiry seem perfunctory and even supercilious.)

we-kêf akhûk ? = *And how is your brother ?*

(It is becoming to ask after male relatives or friends but not after anyone's family as this would include the women, and virtuous women may not have their names dragged into conversation amongst males nor even be thus referred to by implication.)

riglek ! = *Your foot* !

yemînek ! = *Your right* !

(These and such like are street cries warning the foot-passenger to take care of some one riding, driving, or carrying a burden.)

mîn ? = *Who* (*is there*) *?*, *Who is it ?*

(Challenge of sentry, or call of one inside to know who is knocking. The most proper reply is to invoke the name of God (see p. 89) or to bless the Prophet (see p. 89).)

el-wa'd dîn = *A promise is an obligation.*

(Example of nominal sentence formed of two nouns instead of noun and adjective. dîn = "religion," not religious opinions in the European fashion, but the observance of sacred obligations. Muslims do not talk of missionaries "bearing the gospel" but describe them as "introducing the sacred law".)

dînek êy ? = *What is your religion ?*

APPENDIX TO LESSON III

Gentile nouns in -i, fem. iyye : some of these use the fem. as a (collective) plural.

	Singular.	*Plural.*
Abyssinian (so often for negro)	ḥabeshi	ḥabash
Arab	'arabi	'arab
(desert Arab)	bedawi	bedâwi
Copt (Egyptian Christian)	qibṭi	qibṭ
Christian	naṣrâni	naṣâra
	masîḥi	masîḥiyye

(The former term is in more general use, but Christians often prefer the latter.)

	Singular.	*Plural.*
Egyptian	miṣri	miṣriyye
English	inkelîzi	inkelîz
European	firengi	afrang
French	faransâwi	faransîs
German	nimsâwi	nimsâwiyye

(Really this denotes Austrian, the branch of the German race which had earliest contact with the Muslim world. More correctly (but not commonly) the North German is " alamâni ".)

Greek	rûmi	rûm
	yûnâni	yûn

(rûmi = " Roman," i.e. subject of the Byzantine Empire, yunâni = Ionian. The Greek language is called rumi, Latin is firengi.)

Indian	hindi	hunûd
Italian	iṭâliya	ṭalyâni
Jew	yehûdi	yehûd
Muslim	muslim	muslimîn

(Do not use the term " Muhammedan ".)

Persian	'agemi	'agem
	farisi	furs
Syrian	shâmi	shâm
Turk	turki	etrâk
	'usmâni	
	'usmânli (= Turkish horseman)	
Western (Morocco, etc.)	maghribi	maghâribe

Chapter VI

THE FOURTH LESSON—THE SUFFIXED PRONOUNS WITH PREPOSITIONS

(16) The suffixed pronouns may be attached to prepositions and then denote the objective " me ", " thee ", " him ", etc. Thus ma' = " with ", ma'i = " with me ", ma'ek = " with thee ", etc.

List of Commoner Prepositions

'an " with, from ".

'ala " upon ", really 'alay ('alê) and so 'alê- with a suffix, as 'alêk = " upon thee ", 'alêkum = " upon you ", etc. With the 1st sing. -î the suffix becomes -ya, -ye, or -yi (as with abû-) thus 'alêya = " upon me ".

'and " with ".

bi- " in ", bî = " in me ", bek = " in thee " (for bi-ek), buh, bo = " in him ", biha = " in her ", bina = " in us ", etc.

fî " in ", fî = " in me ", fîk = " in thee ", fîh = " in him ", etc.

ila " to, towards ", like 'ala its final -a = -ay and so -ê before suffixes, ilêya = " towards me ", ilêk = " towards thee ", etc.

ka- " like ".

li-fi " to ", lî = " to me ", lik = " to thee ", luh = " to him ", lana = " to us ", lakum = " to you ", lahum = " to them ".

ma‘ "with".
min "from", with suffixes minn-, as minni = "from me", minnek = "from thee", etc.

The prepositions bi-, ka-, li- can only be used as prefixes before nouns or pronouns, the others can stand alone, though still of course before the nouns they govern. Thus we can say fi l-medîne = "in the city", but "to the city", if we use li-, must have the li- joined up as in "li-l-medîne".

(17) Special Use of Fi

The form fîh = "in it" is commonly used in the colloquial as meaning "there is", and so fish as "is there ?" and ma fish "there is not". Thus :—

honak fîh môya = *There is water there* (Of course this can be a question if uttered in an interrogative tone.)
fîsh khubz ? (Eg. ‘êsh) = *Is there any bread ?*
ma fîsh môya = *There is no water*

(18) Special Negative in Syrian Arabic

In Syrian dialect we find mann- (=ma ann-, the ann- being a particle) with the personal suffix used as a negative, thus manni kâtib = "I am not writing", mannek kâtib = "thou art not writing", mannuh kâtib = "he is not writing", etc.

(19) Ways of Expressing "Have"

The preposition ‘and means "with", "in the possession of", and with the personal suffixes this conveys the sense of "have", thus :—

ʻandi = *I have*
ʻandek = *Thou hast*
ʻandik = *Thou* (fem.) *hast*
ʻanduh = *He has*
ʻandiha = *She has*
ʻandine = *We have*
ʻandukum = *You have*
ʻanduhum = *They have.* ʻand-u-hum, -u- by assimilation.

Possession can be represented by li-, ʻand-, or maʻ-. The first of these means " have " in the sense of being the owner, ʻand- is used for smaller things actually in one's possession and maʻ- for movable things which are with one at the moment. Thus " the house belongs to me " = el-bêt li (I am the owner of the house); " have you any books ? " addressed to a shop-keeper = ʻandikum kutub ? Again ownership but of smaller movable articles : " have you your books with you ? " = kutubkum maʻek ?

In such a sentence as " come for a walk with me " the " with " is of course maʻ- as meaning " in my company ".

WORD LIST

ʻabd (ʻebd)	= *slave*
Allâh, -llâh	= *God*
ʻazba*	= *farm*
baʻîd	= *remote*
baqare*	= *cow*
bardân	= *cold* (of persons)
bârid	= *cold* (*of things*; also *of persons* in the sense of irresponsive, indifferent)
dahab	= *gold*
felûs, fulûs	= *money*
fikr	= *thought, opinion*
gamûse*	= *buffalo*
gawâb	= *letter*
ḥâḍir	= *present, ready*
ḥâkim	= *governor*
ḥakîm	= *physician*
ḥamd	= *praise*
ḥaqq	= *right, justice, claim*
ḥurrîye*	= *liberty*
izn (idhn)	= *permission*
kelâm	= *speech*
khâṭir	= *danger*
leʻab	= *sport, play*
mâhir	= *skilful*
maṭar	= *rain*
sâʻa*	= *hour, watch*

EXERCISE

(1) min ên entum ?—'abadkum min el-Higâz	= **Where are you from ?—Your servants are from the Hijaz.**
(2) fîsh 'andukum môya ?—aiwa, ahe môya ketîr	= **Have you any water ?—Yes, here is plenty of water.**
(3) 'azbetek fên ?—el-'azba betâ'eti hiya qarîbe min hêna	= **Where is your farm ?—My farm is near here.**
(4) 'andek baqare ?—aiwa, ahe el-baqare betâ'eti	= **Have you a cow ?—Yes, here is my cow.**
(5) 'andek felûs ? — ma'ek felûs ?	= **Have you any money ?—Have you any money with you ?**
(6) la, ma fîsh ma'i felûs	= **No, I have no money with me.**
(7) el-môya bârid ?—la, -el môya mush bârid	= **Is the water cold ?—No, the water is not cold.**
(8) 'andi sâ'a min dahab	= **I have a gold watch.**
(9) fi fikri sâ'atek mush min dahab	= **I think your watch is not gold.**
(10) el-ḥakîm ḥâḍir ?—la, ya sîdi, ma fîsh ḥakîm fi beledna	= **Is the doctor present ?—No, Sir, there is no doctor in our village.**
(11) mîn el-khawâge 'ala yemînek ?—el-khawâge hûwa el-ḥâkim	= **Who is the gentleman on your right ?—The gentleman is the governor.**
(12) kêr akhûkum ?—akhûna huwa marîḍ 'ala khâṭir	= **How is your brother ?—Our brother is dangerously ill.**
(13) fîh ma'ek sikkîn ?—aiwa, ma'i sikkîn	= **Have you a knife with you ?—Yes, I have a knife.**

(14) li ḥaqq ʻalêk	= **I have a claim against you.**
(15) ʻandek waqt ?—ma ʻandîsh waqt li-l-leʻab	= **Have you any time ?—I have no time for play.**
(16) ʻandek akhbâr ?	= **Have you any news ?**
(17) mush li khôf	= **I have no fear.**
(18) Maḥmûd fên ?—huwa fi l-gâmiʻ el-azhar maʻ abûh	= **Where is Mahmud ?—He is in the al-Azhar mosque with his father.**
(19) li kelâm maʻkum	= **I want to have a word with you.**
(20) ʻala l-bâb ḥammâl we-maʻuh ṣandûq	= **There is a porter at the door and he has a box with him.**
(21) ʻand mîn el-ḥaqq ?—el-ḥaqq ʻandi, el-ḥaqq ʻalêk	= **Who is in the right ?—I am in the right, you are incorrect.**
(22) bi-abûya ente	= **You are like a father to me.**
(23) ʻan iznek (idhnek)	= **With your leave.**

(On taking a seat, on taking leave, on going away from the company for any purpose, and on entering a latrine in which case the expression is a propitiatory remark addressed to the evil spirits which haunt such places, the more necessary because guardian angels do not accompany men there but wait for them outside.)

(24) ya li-r-rigâl	= **Help, O men (= O to the men).**
(25) lêsh ente hêna ?	= **Why (= for what) are you here ?**
(26) fi Maṣr ma fîsh ḥurriya	= **There is no liberty in Egypt.**
(27) fîsh ʻêsh ?—la, ya sîdi, ma fîsh ʻêsh	= **Is there any bread ?—No, sir, there is no bread.**
(28) ahe gawâb li-ḥaḍretek	= **Here is a letter for your honour.**

(29) bedelek hiye ba'îde min hêna ? = **Is your town far from here?**

(30) ya salâm, fi fikri ana marîḍ = **Good heavens, I think I am ill.**

(31) eṭ-ṭarîq ila medîneti huwa ṭawîl qawi = **It is a long way to my city.**

(32) enta mâlek = **What is the matter? (Syria). Mind your own business (Egypt).**

(33) ma'alêsh = **No matter.**

(34) honak fîh maqâm = **There is a holy place there (Damascus).**

(35) salâm 'alêkum—we-'alêkum salâm = **Peace be on you.—And on you be peace.**

(Greeting of one Muslim to another. It should not be used by Muslims to unbelievers or by non-Muslims at all. If addressed by a non-Muslim to a Muslim it should not be returned. Non-Muslims use some such form as :—)

(36) nehârkum sa'îd—nehârkum sa'îd we-mubârak = **May your day be prosperous and blessed.**

(It is very seemly, though not necessary, to return a compliment with interest.)

(37) kêf ḥâlkum ? =
ezayyek ? (Egypt, familiar) =
êsh ḥâlek ? (Syria) = **How are you?**

(38) el-ḥamdu li-llâh = **Praise be to God.**

(The -u properly (but not always) given at the end of ḥamd- is the classical nominative termination. Only the tone of voice shows whether this is thanks for good health or resignation in ill-health. To say "I am well" is unlucky, as it has a tone of boasting and invites the attention of malevolent spirits, whilst to say "I am ill" savours of petulance.)

(39) khâṭirek.—ma'a (ma') s-selâme *or* awaqâtek sa'îde	= **(Guest about to depart says) "Your permission.—(Go) with peace** *or* **May your times be prosperous".**
(40) ma 'anduhumsh 'êsh	= **They have no bread.**
(41) 'andekshe ḥeṭeb li-l-bî' ?	= **Have you any fuel for sale?**
(42) ya khângi, kâm el-ḥisâb ?	= **Landlord, how much is the bill?**

(-gi is a Turkish ending, khan-gi means " man of the khan (inn).")

(43) ya khângi, 'êsh 'andek li-l-'asha (li-l-ghadâ) ?	= **Landlord, have you anything for supper (dinner)?**

Chapter VII

THE FIFTH LESSON—THE DEMONSTRATIVES AND RELATIVE

(I) The Demonstrative

Form (i) "*this*", "*these*".

In the form and use of the demonstrative there is a marked difference between the various dialects, and when such is the case it is generally a saving of time to begin with the classical form and trace the way in which the dialects diverge from it.

The classical "this" may appear as dha, or reinforced by the prefix hâ-, which probably was at first an emphatic as ha-dha. From these we get:—

	Singular.		*Plural.*
	Masculine.	*Feminine.*	
(*a*)	dhâ	(ti)	('ulâ)
(*b*)	hâdhâ	hâdhî	ha'ulâ

These may be used (1) as demonstrative pronouns, as hâdhâ kitâb = "this is a book", hâdhî bint = "this is a girl", such a pronoun being naturally defined; or (2) as demonstrative adjectives attached to nouns which must then be defined, as hâdhâ l-kitâb "this book", hâdhî l-bint "this girl", etc., used thus adjectivally it is necessarily followed by the defining article.

The Dialect of 'Iraq follows this very closely, save that it discards the rather peculiar plural and forms a new one from the singular stem, thus:—

hâdhâ hâdhî hâdhôl

These are used (1) as demonstrative pronouns, hâdhâ bêt = "this is a house", hâdhî bint = "this is a girl", etc., but (2) used as adjectives they tend to contract with the definite article which invariably follows and so make:—

hadhel hadhil hadhôl

The plural hadhôl is as before, but the two singular forms include the article, thus hadhel-bet = "this house", hadhil-bint = "this girl" and the final -l assimilates like that in the article, thus hadher-rigâl "this man", etc. Both these singular forms can be further contracted into hel as hel-kitâb = "this book", her-rigâl = "this man", etc., and this hel can even be used for the plural provided it refers to things not persons. Thus:—

hadhel (hel) kitâb ṭayyib = *This book is good*
hadhil (hel) bint marîḍa = *This girl is ill*
hadha kitâb ṭayyib = *This is a good book*
hadhi dâr kebîra = *This is a large house*

Very much the same holds good with Maghrabi (Moroccan) Arabic where we find *sing. masc.* hadha, *fem.* hadhi, *plur.* hadhum; but no contraction with the article takes place.

In the dialect of Syria naturally dh becomes d but otherwise the same forms are maintained, thus:—

hada hadi hadol

These are used (*a*) as pronouns, as hada kitâb = "this is a book", hadi bint = "this is a girl", hadôl 'arab = "these are Arabs"; (*b*) as adjectives where they may either stand before the article or contract with it to hal, thus hada l-kitâb *or* hal-kitâb "this book", hadi l-bint = "this girl", *or* hal-bint, hadôl el-'arab *or* hal-'arab = "these Arabs", the hal being capable of free use with either gender or number, though it is more commonly found with the singular. The

-l of hal assimilates in the usual way, thus har-râgul = "this man", has-sâ'a = "this hour", etc.

In Syrian Arabic we also hear (rarely) the form *sing. masc.* hai-da, *fem.* hai-di.

In Egyptian Arabic the ha- prefix is missing altogether and so we get—

sing. masc. dâ *fem.* dî *plur.* dôl

These forms are used (*a*) as pronouns, thus dâ bêt = "this is a house", dî shughli ṣâ'abe = "this is a hard task", êy dôl = "what are these?"; (*b*) as adjectives they *follow* the noun which must have the article before it, as el-kitâb dâ = "this book", el-bint dî = "this girl", el-'arab dôl = "these Arabs". If the noun has a descriptive adjective attached the demonstrative may follow the noun itself or the descriptive and so for "this great man" we can say er-râgil dâ el-kebîr *or* er-râgil el-kebîr dâ, and for "this little girl" either el-bint dî eṣ-ṣaghîre *or* el-bint eṣ-ṣaghîre dî.

Form (ii) "*this* (*is*)", *etc.*

This is a special (and occasional) use of the ha- which we have already seen prefixed to the demonstrative dha in hadha ; it occurs :—

(1) In Palestinian Arabic as hei (heiy-) "here is", which can take the personal suffixes. With the suffix of the 1st sing. a "supporting n" is used, as heini = "here am I", with the other persons heiy- is used, as heiyek = "here you are", heiyo = "here is he", etc.

(2) In Egyptian Arabic it appears as a-, which can only be used with a suffix of the 3rd sing. as aho, ahe: properly the first of these is masculine, the second feminine, but this distinction is no longer carefully observed: fên kitâbi?—aho kitâbek = "where is my book?—Here is your book".

Form (iii) "*that*", "*those*".

"That" is formed from "this" by adding the "k of the remote", thus :—

classical *sing. masc.* dhâk *fem.* tilk *plur.* 'ulâ'ik

In the dialect of 'Iraq we get (by adding -k to the "nearer",) this :—

hadhâk	hadhîk	hadhôlak
	hadhîch	

The reduction of -k to -ch (like the ch- in "cheese") we have already observed in the suffixed pronoun (cf. p. 40 above). These forms can be used as pronouns or adjectives, thus hadhak bêt = "that is a house", hadhâk el-bêt = "that house", etc. The plural hadhôlak must be used with persons, but for things in the plural it is permitted to use the feminine hadhîk, hadhîch.

Syrian dialect uses hâk for all genders and numbers but permits an alternative haidik for the singular and plural *masc.* hadôlak, *fem.* hadôlik, but the use of these forms is commoner in Palestine and is (perhaps) a mark of Palestinian dialect.

Egyptian Arabic uses dîk, dâk, for all, but permits also :—

sing. masc. dukha *fem.* dikha *plur.* dukham, dukhamma

In Syria and in 'Iraq this demonstrative, like "this, these" has to be placed before the noun when used adjectivally and the noun must have the article, thus hâk el-kitâb mufîd = "that book is useful", etc., but in Egyptian it is placed after the noun defined by the article, as er-ragil dak huwa tagir = "that man is a merchant", etc. It is a marked peculiarity of Egyptian that even the ha- is placed at the end, and so we get duk-ha, etc.

We have given the forms for both "this" and "that", but in fact Arabic often uses "this" where we would have

" that ", thus da o da = " this or that " and very often the hada, da, of Arabic can best be translated in English by " that" rather than " this ".

SUMMARY OF THE DEMONSTRATIVE FORMS.

	Classical.	'Iraq.	Syria.	Egypt.
(i) " this "	dha ti 'ula	— — —	— — —	da di dol
	hadha hadhi ha'ûla	hadha hadhi hadhol	hada hadi hadol	— — —
(ii) " this "	(ha-)	—	hei (heiy-)	a-
(iii) " that "	dhak tilk 'ulâ'ik	hadhak hadhik (-ch) hadholak	hak haidik {hadolak {hadolik	{dak dukha {dik dikha dukham

EXAMPLES

(Chiefly Egyptian)

(1) el-bâb dâ maftûḥ ? = *Is that door open ?*

(2) dî lokânda ṭayyib ? = *Is this a good hotel ?*

(3) el-lokânda dî mush ṭalîq li-ḥaḍretek = *That hotel is not suitable for for your honour*

(4) el-ôḍa dî neḍîfe ? = *Is this room clean ?*

(5) aiwa, el-ôḍa dî neḍîfe ketîr = *Yes, this room is very clean*

(6) fi fikri hâdi l-lokânda mush neḍîfa = *I think this hotel is not clean*

(7) na'am, ya sîdi, hal-lokânda neḍîfa = *Yes, sir, this hotel is clean*

(8) da ḥiṣân ḍa'îf = *That is a weak horse*

(9) el-ḥiṣân da ḍa'îf = *That horse is weak*

(10) ed-darsi da ṣa'ab qawi = *This lesson is very difficult*
(11) di shughli ṣa'abe = *This is a hard task*
(12) lek dâr fi l-beled di ? = *Have you a house in this town ?*
(13) mîn el-khawâge da ? = *Who is that gentleman ?*
(14) el-khawâge da hûwa el-qonṣul faransâwi = *That gentleman is the French consul*
(15) êy di ? = *What is this ?*
(16) êy da fi miqṭafek ? = *What is that in your basket ?*
(17) hada nawâri aṣli (Syr.) = *This man is a thorough gipsy*
(18) da kelâm mufîd = *That is a useful remark*
(19) hadôl el-'arab (el-'arab dôl) ḥarâmiye = *Those Arabs are thieves*
(20) en-nâs dôl hum bedâwiye min es-Sînâ = *These men are bedwin from Sinai*
(21) er-râgil dâk hûwa et-tâgir el-'agemi = *That man is the Persian merchant*
(22) es-sitt di hîya inkelîzi = *That lady is English* (E.)
(23) el-inkelîzi da hûwa min el-Hind = *That Englishman is from India* (E.)
(24) hada asad = *This is a lion* (S.)
(25) hal-asad = *This lion* (S.)
(26) hada l-bortuqân ṭaiyib = *This orange is good* (S.)
(27) hal-bortuqân mush ṭayyib = *This orange is no good* (S.)
(28) hada bortuqân ṭayyib = *This is a good orange* (S.)
(29) da hûwa el-mudîr = *That is the mudir* (E.)
(30) di hîya s-sitt Zeinab = *This is the lady Zeinab* (E.)
(31) hadha kitâb mufîd = *This is a useful book* (I.)
(32) hel-kitâb mufîd = *This book is useful* (I.)

(II) The Relative

In 'Iraq, Syria, Palestine, and Egypt colloquial Arabic uses illi, elli, as the relative, occasionally ma. The relative refers normally to a defined antecedent, with an antecedent undefined the relative may be altogether omitted or, if it is a thing, ma can be used.

It is sometimes said that Arabic has no relative: that is not true, but it must be admitted that the Arabic relative is very restricted in its use. One noteworthy peculiarity is that it is nominative only and so can only express the possessive or objective by means of a suffixed pronoun following: thus for "the man whose horse (came, etc.) . . ." we must say "the man who his horse (came) . . ." = er-râgil illi ḥiṣânuh . . .: for "I saw the man whom you saw" it has to be "I saw the man who you saw him", etc.

el-kitâb illi 'andekum = *The book which you have*

(This is quite straightforward because "have" is expressed "is with you".)

el-kitâb illi ketebtûh = *The book which I wrote* (= which I wrote it)

In many cases, however, Arabic does not express the relative where it would be needed in English, thus :—

râgil gâ = *The man who came*
râgil huwa ṣâḥibi = *The man who is my friend*
marrêt bi-râgil abûh nâyim = *I passed by the man, his father was asleep* (= whose father . . .)

Very often the article with a participle serves for a relative clause, as el-mu'menîn = "the believers" = "they who believe", etc.

WORD LIST

ayye ? = *of what kind ?*
dars = *lesson*
gâz = *petrol*
khôf = *fear*
kitâb (*plur.* kutub) = *book*
lêl, lêle* (masc. or fem.) = *night*
ma'rife = *knowledge, sense*
meshghûl = *busy*
mufîd = *useful*
mehâr = *day* (not night), en-nehâr da = *to-day* (Eg.).
otomôbil = *automobile* (Fr.)
qalam = *pen*
qonṣul = *consul*
râgil (*plur.* rigâl, but cf. p. 69 below) = *man, men*
sirag = *lamp*
ṭalîq = *suitable*
ṭarabêza = *table* (Greek)
yôm (*pl.* aiyâm) = *day* (*twenty-four hours*)
el-yom = *to-day* ('Iraq)
hal-yôm = *to-day* (Syr.)
zêt = *oil*
mush kida ? (= ka-da) (kida also as kiza, cf. p. 11) = ***is it not so ?***
da l-waqt da = ***it is already*** . . . (*this is this time* (*that*) . . .)
we-fi aiyâm dôl . . . = *and in those days . . .*

EXERCISE A

(The use of the demonstrative is one of the few cases in which there is a material difference between the colloquial of Egypt, Syria, and 'Iraq, and therefore this first exercise illustrates the way in which the demonstrative is employed in these various dialects, the English of (I) being rendered according to each in the three sections following.)

(I) (1) This is a large house. This house is large. This large house. (2) This is a small house. This house is small. This small house. (3) What is this?—this is a pen. And what is this ?—this is my book. (4) Is this book large ?—no, this book is small. (5) Where are these books ?—these books are on the table.

(II) *Egyptian.*—(1) da bêt kebîr—el-bêt da kebîr—el-bêt el-kebîr da. (2) di dâr ṣaghîre—ed-dâr di ṣaghîre—ed dâr di eṣ-ṣaghîre. (3) êy da ?—da qalam—we-êy da (w-êy da) ?—da kitâbi. (4) el-kitâb da kebîr ?—la, el-kitâb

(ʻa ṣaghîr. (5) fên el-kutub dôl ?—el-kutub dôl ʻala ṭ-ṭarabêza daṭ-ṭarabêza).

(III) *Syrian.*—(1) hâda bêt kebîr—hâda l-bêt (hal-bêt) kebîr—hâl-bêt el-kebîr. (2) hâdi dâr ṣaghîre—hâd-dâr ṣaghîre—hâd-dâr eṣ-ṣaghîre. (3) êy hâda ?—hâda qalam—w-êy hâda ?—hâda kitâbi. (4) hâl-kitâb kebir ?—la, hâl-kitâb ṣaghîr. (5) ên hâl-kutub ?—hâl-kutub ʻala ṭ-ṭarabêza.

(IV) *Iraqi.*—(1) hadha bêt kebîr—hadhel-bêt kebîr—hadhel-bêt el-kebîr. (2) hâdhi dâr ṣaghîre—hâdhed-dâr ṣaghîre—hâdhed-dâr eṣ-ṣaghîre. (3) êy hâdha ?—hâdha qalam—w-êy hâdha ?—hâdha kitâbi. (4) hel-kitâb kebîr ?—la, hel-kitâb ṣaghîr. (5) wên hadhol-kutub ?—hadhol kutub ʻala ṭ-ṭarabeza.

EXERCISE B

(1) ayye el-kitâb da (hâdha l-kitâb, hal-kitâb) ? = **What kind of book is this ?**

(2) el-kitâb da mufîd = **This is a useful book.**

(3) ed-darsi da ṣaʻab ?—aiwa, ed-darsi da ṣaʻab ketîr = **Is this lesson hard ?—Yes, this lesson is very hard.**

(4) esh-shughli da ṣaʻab ?—aiwa da shughli ṣaʻab = **Is this task difficult ?—Yes, this task is difficult.**

(5) da nehâr leṭîf ?—en-nehâr da leṭîf = **Is it a fine day ?—To-day is fine.**

(6) er-râgil da hûwa ʻarabi min el-Higâz = **This man is an Arab from the Hijaz.**

(7) er-rigâl dol hum ʻarab min es-sînâ = **These men are Arabs from Sinai.**

(8) el-kelâm da mufîd qawi = **That statement is very useful.**

(9) mafîsh zêt fi s-sirag da = **There is no oil in this lamp.**

(10) el-ḥakîm da hûwa meshghûl qawi ?—la, hûwa keslân ketîr	= **Is this doctor very busy ?—No, he is very indolent.**
(11) en-nehâr fi ṣ-ṣêf hûwa ṭawîl	= **The day is long in summer.**
(12) el-lêle di hîya ṭawîle ṭawîle	= **This night is very long.**
(13) el-ḥâkim el-kebîr dâk hûwa el-yôm marîḍ 'ala khâṭir	= **That chief governor is to-day seriously ill.**
(14) fi r-râgil da mafîsh khôf	= **In this man is no fear.**
(15) fi l-otomôbil betâ'i mafîsh gâz	= **There is no petrol in my automobile.**
(16) fi r-râgil da ma'rife kêtîr	= **There is much good sense in this man.**
(17) êy di ?—di gâz. w-êy di ?—di môya.	= **What is this ?—It is petrol. And this ?—It is water.**
(18) el-kitâb da kebîr, we-l-kitâb da ṣaghîr, mush kida ?	= **This book is big, and that book is small, is it not so ?**
(19) fên el-kutub dôl ?—el-kutub dôl hum 'ala ṭ-ṭarâbeza	= **Where are these books ?—These books are on the table.**
(20) el-walad eṣ-ṣaghîr en-nehâr da fên ?—el-walad eṣ-ṣaghîr hûwa ma' abûh fi l-bêt betâ'uh	= **Where is the little boy to-day ? — To-day the little boy is at home with his father.**
(21) has-sâ'a hîya ṭayyib mush ketîr	=**This watch is not very good.**
(22) el-bêt da lek ?—aiwa, el-bêt da li	= **Does this house belong to you ?—Yes, this house is mine.**

(23) er-râgil da hûwa inkelîzi = **This man is English.**

(24) el-inkelîzi da hûwa el-qonṣul = **This Englishman is the consul.**

(25) dîk huwa el-qonṣul el-inkelîzi = **That is the English consul.**

(26) el-yehûdi dîk hûwa el-qonṣul el-nimsâwi = **That Jew is the German Consul.**

(27) hâdha l-bedâwi hûwa min el-Ḥigâz = **That Bedawi is from the Higaz.**

(28) di lokânda ṭayyibe ?—la, el-lokânda di mush ṭalîq li-ḥaḍretek = **Is this a good hotel?—No, that hotel is not fit for your honour.**

(29) lokânda neḍîfe fên ?—'ala fikri el-lokânda di hîye neḍîfe = **Where is there a clean hotel?—In my opinion this is a clean hotel.**

(30) aiwa, ya khawâge, el-lokânda di neḍîfe giddan = **Yes, sir, this is a very clean hotel.**

(31) êsh el-kalâm da ? = **What is the meaning of this? (=what is this saying?)**

(32) da l-waqt el-ezân (edân, edhân) = **This is the time for the call to prayer (it is already . . .)**

(33) da lek ? = **Is this yours?**

(34) êsh min shâgare di ? = **What kind of tree is this?**

(35) el-kitâb da kebîr 'an dûkha = **This book is bigger than that one (= is large above that one).**

(36) 'andakum kutub inkelîzi ? = **Have you any English books?**

(37) aiwa, ya khawâge, 'andi = **Yes, sir, I have.**

(38) ayye el-kutub illi 'andakum ? = **What sort of books have you? (= what sort the books which you have?)**

Chapter VIII

THE SIXTH LESSON—THE PLURALS OF NOUNS

Formation of the Plural

In Arabic there are two kinds of plurals which are commonly termed the "strong" and the "weak" or "broken" plurals. The former are formed by adding plural terminations to the stem just as English adds plural -s, -es, to the stem in such words as "book, books", "house, houses", etc.—the weak or broken plurals are those formed by internal change similar to that employed in English in forming such plurals as "mouse, mice", "man, men", etc.

Strong Plurals Masculine

Strong plurals of masculine nouns are formed by adding -în to the stem, thus muʿallim "teacher", muʿallimîn "teachers" —Muslim, Muslimîn, etc. Strong plurals of this kind are formed with nouns (adjectives, etc.), which were originally participles of verbs, as shâṭir "crafty", pl. shâṭirîn—mablûl "wet", mablûlîn, etc.; with words of the form qattâl denoting trades such as ḥaddâd "smith", ḥaddâdîn, etc. A selection of some of the commonest words of this kind will be found in the word list below.

Strong Plurals Feminine

The strong plural of the feminine is formed by changing the -a, -e, of the singular which, as we have already noted (p. 24), really represents -at, -et, into ât- and in this plural the final -t does not fall away. It must be noted, however, that not all feminines ending -a, -e, in the singular make this strong plural, there are many which make broken plurals instead : on the other hand, there are feminine nouns not ending in -a, -e, in the singular which nevertheless make their plural by adding -ât. Thus :—

ḥara	= " street "	pl. ḥarât
muslima	= " Muslim woman "	muslimât
gawâb	= " letter "	gawâbât

Especially it must be noted here that the singular -a, -e does not always denote a feminine singular, but it is sometimes used to form the noun of the individual from the noun of species, as tîn = " fig, figs ", tîna = " a single fig ", in such cases of course the plural is simply the noun without the -a, -e, used to form the name of the individual.

The Dual

A special termination in -ên is used to denote the dual, i.e. two things. This is chiefly used for words which naturally denote things which are in pairs, thus îd " hand ", îdên " two hands ", etc., but it is used (though not consistently) for other instances of twos, as sâ'a " hour ", sâ'atên " two o'clock ", etc. There is no " weak " alternative for the dual and the same termination is used for masculine and feminine nouns.

Broken Plurals

Broken plurals are formed by internal change, such as kitâb = " book ", kutub = " books ", kelb = " dog ", kilâb = " dogs ", etc., some of these plurals adding terminations such as -ân, or prefixes such as a- but preserving the three (or four) basal consonants of the stem. When the singular has more than four letters (i.e. consonants and *long* vowels) the plural always reduces the number to four.

The broken plurals are fairly numerous and usually prove a difficulty to the learned, though by no means so serious a one as at first appears. The various "measures" must be found from the dictionary or from word-lists. There is indeed a system, but little if any time will be saved by trying to learn it. For example, plurals of the measure qital are formed from singulars, of measures qatl, qitl, qutl, qatal, qatul, qatle*, qatale*, qutle*, qatîl, qâtil; and singulars of the measure qatl form plurals of the measures qitla*, qitala*, qutûl, qutûla*, qitâl, qatîl; so the different forms of the singular do not regularly correspond with fixed plural forms. But many of the forms given in the lists of the grammarians are very rare in colloquial speech so that it is best, perhaps, to content oneself with learning the plural forms as they occur. In the word-lists following the plurals are given in brackets after the singular. Some nouns, of course, do not admit any plural, e.g. shems "sun", and in some cases there are alternative forms of broken plural and (occasionally) one dialect prefers one of these whilst other dialects prefer another.

The broken plurals are treated as feminine singulars, no doubt because they were originally collectives. Thus:—

el-gibal hiye ʻaliyye = *The mountains are lofty.*

Those, however, which denote males may be treated as masculine plural or (less commonly) as feminine singular, as:—

er-rigâl ṣâliḥîn = *The men are honest.*

This lesson does not lead to any very important principles as to the use of word forms, but is chiefly concerned with matters of vocabulary. Most of our attention therefore will be given to the lists following. First we shall give lists of common words forming strong plurals, then certain exceptional forms, and finally some lists of the more usual broken plurals, these latter being continued for the next two lessons. After that it will be necessary to note the broken plurals as they occur and finally to prepare one's own lists and learn them as vocabularies.

WORD LIST

(*a*) Masculine Nouns forming Strong Plurals in -în.

(i) Participial and kindred forms.

mâhir	= *skilful*	nâfi'	= *useful.*
mablûl	= *wet*	shâṭir	= *crafty*
mabsûṭ	= *happy*	wâsi'	= *spacious*
muslim	= *Muslim*		

And the adjectives in -ân such as keslân, etc. (cf. p. 37).

(ii) Trades, etc., of measure qattâl.

bayyâ'	= *dealer*	khayyâṭ	= *tailor*
ḥaddâd	= *smith*	naggâr	= *carpenter*
ḥallâq	= *barber*	sammâk	= *fisherman*
ḥammâl	= *porter, carrier*	ṣarrâf	= *money changer*
khabbâz	= *baker*	ṣayyâd	= *hunter (fisher)*
khaddâm	= *servant*		

(*b*) Strong Feminine Plurals in -ât.

bûsta*	= *post office*	ḥâra* [1]	= *street*
gâra*	= *neighbour*	lokânda*	= *hotel*
gawâb, *pl.* akhawat	= *letter*	maḥaṭṭa*	= *railway station*

(*c*) Anomalous Feminine Forms.

bint, *pl.* banât	= *girl, daughter*	umm, *pl.* ummahât	= *mother*
ukht, *pl.* akhawât	= *sister*		

(*d*) Broken Plurals of form qitâl.

beled, *pl.* bilâd	= *town, country*	ḥabl, *pl.* ḥibâl	= *rope*
dâr,[2] *pl.* diyâr	= *house*	kelb, *pl.* kilâb	= *dog*
farkhe,* *pl.* firâkh	= *fowl*	râgil, *pl.* rigâl	= *man* [3]
gebel, *pl.* gibâl	= *mountain*	rîḥ,[2] *pl.* riyâḥ	= *wind*
gemel, *pl.* ginâl	= *camel*		

(*e*) Broken Plurals of the form qutul.

kitâb, *pl.* kutub	= *book*	ṭarîq, *pl.* ṭuruq	= *road*
medîne*, *pl.* mudun	= *city*		

[1] Ḥâra really denotes a quarter of the town, the more correct name for a street in the mo lern sense is shâri' (*pl.* shawâri').

[2] It will be noted that the plural restores the original consonants which, if weak, often are absorbed in the neighbouring vowel in the singular, thus rih = riyh, and dar = dayr, etc.

[3] Ir. also rigagil, riyayil which Van Ess notes as "vulgar".

EXERCISE

(1) er-rigâl dôl hum ḥaddâdîn	=	**Those men are smiths.**
(2) el-ḥarât tawîle	=	**The streets are long.**
(3) el-ḥaddâdin dôl (hadôl el-ḥaddâdîn, hal-ḥaddâdîn) hum keslânîn qawi	=	**Those smiths are very idle.**
(4) fi l-medîne el-qarîbe ḥallâqin ketîr	=	**There are many barbers in the neighbouring city.**
(5) el-beyût illi fi l-medîne di (hadi (hadhi) l-medine) hîya ʻaliyye ketîr	=	**The houses in this city are very lofty.**
(6) fi l-medîne di lokândât ketîre	=	**There are many inns in this city.**
(7) en-nehârât fi ṣ-ṣêf ṭawîle waqi	=	**In the summer the days are very long.**
(8) fi l-mudun el-kebîre ḥammâlîn ketîr	=	**In large towns there are many porters.**
(9) mîn er-râgil da ?—huwa khaddâmi	=	**Who is that man?— He is my servant.**
(10) fîsh khayyât fi l-beled di (hal-beled, hadhi l-beled) ? —naʻam, ya khawâge, fîh	=	**Is there a tailor in this village?—Yes, sir, there is.**
(11) fên el-maḥaṭṭa ?—el-maḥaṭṭa hiya fi sh-shâriʻ dak ʻala yemînek	=	**Where is the railway station? —The railway station is in that street to your right.**
(12) el-ʻarab dôl (hal-ʻarab, hadhol el-ʻarab) ʻala fikri hum ṣayyâdîn	=	**Those Arabs in my opinion are hunters.**
(13) eṭ-ṭurûq illi fi beledek mush wâsiʻe	=	**The roads in your country are not wide.**

(14) min ên er-rigâl dôl ?—hum 'arab we-hum ḥammâlîn min el-Ḥigâz	= **Where are those men from ?—They are Arabs and they are carriers from the Hijaz.**
(15) fi Maṣr malik dilwaqt	= **There is a king now in Egypt.**
(16) mîn el-wilâd dôl ?—ya sîdi, hum wilâdna	= **Who are those children ?—Sir, they are my children.**
(17) ahe gawâbât li-ḥaḍretek	= **Here are letters for your honour.**
(18) fi l-maḥaṭṭa ḥammâl ?—aiwa, ya jkhawâge, fi l-maḥaṭṭa ḥammâlîn ketîr qawi	= **Is there a porter at the station ?—Yes, sir, there are many porters at the station.**
(19) 'andukum kutub inkelîzi ?—na'am, ya khawâge, 'andena	= **Have you any English books ?—Yes, sir, we have.**
(20) ayye el-kutub illi 'andekum ?	= **What kind of books have you ?**
(21) 'andek gâz li-otomôbili ?—la, ya sîdi, ma fîsh gâz fi l-beled di	= **Have you petrol for my automobile ? — No, sir, there is no petrol in this town.**
(22) fîsh ṣarrâf fi hal-medîne ?—na'am, fih ṣarrâfîn fi sh-shâri' 'ala shemâlek	= **Is there a money changer in this town ? — Yes, there are money changers in the street to your left.**
(23) fên lokânda ṭayyibe fi l-beled di ?	= **Where is there a good inn in this town ?**
(24) fîh lokândât we-lâkin hîye mush ṭayyibe.	= **There are inns but they are not good.**

Chapter IX

THE SEVENTH LESSON—THE NUMERALS

The Cardinal Numbers

1 "One," masc. wâḥid, fem. waḥde ('Iraq also waḥida). This word is also used for "only", the indefinite "a (certain)".

2 etnên, also t'nên (Syr.), ithnên ('Iraq); here as usual the original "th" is preserved in 'Iraq but becomes "t" in Egypt and Syria. The termination -ên is dual and that termination alone often suffices to denote "two", thus sâ'a (= sâ'at) "hour", sâ'atên = "two o'clock", etc.

3–10. The numerals "three" to "ten" have each two forms, one masculine the other in -a, -e (-at, -et) feminine, but in the colloquial speech the genders are no longer observed, usually the -a, -e form (properly feminine) is used before a word beginning with a consonant, the masculine before one beginning with a vowel, thus khamse buyut = "five houses", khams aiyam = "five days".

3 talât, talâte.
4 arba', arba'a.
5 khams (khamas) khamse.
6 sitt, sitte.
7 seba', seb'a.
8 temân, temâniye.
9 tisa' (tis'), tis'e.
10 'asher, 'ashere.

In 3 and 8 the t- represents original th- and so in 'Iraq we find the more correct forms—3 thalâth, thalâthe, 8 thamân, thamaniya. The t- in 8 is itself the original form, and so does not produce th- in 'Iraq.

11–19. The decimal numbers are formed by combining the units with 'asher "ten", thus:—

11 ḥad'asher.
12 etn'asher ('Iraq, ethn'asher).
13 talat'asher ('Iraq, thalath'asher).
14 arba't'asher.
15 khamsast'asher.
16 sitt'asher.
17 seba't'asher.
18 tamant'asher ('Iraq, thamant asher).
19 tis'at'asher.
20 For "twenty" the plural of "ten" is used, thus 'ashrîn.

30–90. The plurals of the units, thus:—

30 talâthîn (thalâthîn).
40 arba'în, etc.

With these the units are used first and connected with the tens by we- "and", thus 21 = wâḥid we-'ashrîn, 25 = khamas we-'ashrîn, etc.

100 mîye, mîyat, mît.
200 dual of 100, mîtên.
300 tultemîye (thulthemiye).
400 rub'emîye.
500 khumsemîye.
600 suttemîye.
700 sub'emîye.
800 tumnemîye.
900 tus'emîye.
1000 alf.

2000 alfên.
3000 telat alâf.
4000 arba't alâf, etc.
377 = tultemîye we-sab'a we-sab'în, etc.

The numerals 3 to 10 take the accompanying nouns in the plural, but after this the nouns are in the singular, thus :—

one book = kitâb.
two books = kitâbên (dual).
three books = telâte kutub.
twenty books = 'ashrîn kitâb (noun in sing.).

For addition we use we- "and", thus etnên we-telâte = "two plus three"; for subtraction, min "from", thus etnên min telâte = "two from three (three minus two)"; for multiplication, fi "in", as etnên fi telâte = "twice three"; division, 'ala as temânye 'ala etnên = "eight divided by two".

"half" = nuṣṣ.

The Ordinal Numbers

1st awal (awwal, owal), *fem.* awale, owale.

The succeeding numbers are formed on the measure qatil, *fem.* qalte.

2nd tâni, taniye.
3rd tâlit (thalith), talte (thalthe).
4th râbi', rab'e.
5th khâmis, khamse.
6th sâdis, sadse.
7th sâbi', sab'e.
8th tâmin, tamne.
9th tâsi', tas'e.
10th 'âshir, 'ashre.

(The original "six" was sid-, which has become sit- by assimilation to the (feminine) -t ending so that in the ordinal "6th" the true stem appears.)

The word tâni is also used in the sense of "another", and as an adverb meaning "again".

NOTES

(*a*) *Price.*

kâm, bi-kâm = "how much ?"
qadd, si'r, taman = "price".
(tamm = "complete")

"how much is this ?" =
- bi-kâm da ? (how much this ?)
- bi-qaddesh ey ? (at what price ?)
- tamanuh kam ? (how much its price ?)
- qaddesh es-si'r ? (how much is the price ?)

(*b*) *Time, etc.*

es-sa'a kâm ? = "what time is it ?"
kam sene 'umrek ? = "what is your age ?" (how many years your age ?)
kam sene luh ? = "how old is he ?" (how many years has he ?)

(*c*) *Arithmetical processes.*

Addition, we- or ila :	telâta we- (ila) arba'a	= "three plus four".
Subtraction, min :	khamse min sab'a	= "seven minus five".
Multiplication, fi :	khamse fi sab'a	= "five times seven".
Division, 'ala :	'ashrîn 'ala khamse	= "twenty divided by five".

Proportion, nasba . . . ila . . . ka-nasba . . . ila . . ., nasba arba'a ila temân ka-nasba talata ila sitt = 4 : 8 :: 3 : 6.

EXAMPLES

bi-kam da ?	= *How much is this ?*
bi-talât qurûsh	= *Three piastres*
da ghâli bi-s-si'r da	= *It is dear at that price*
la, da rakhîṣ giddan bi-s-si'r da	= *No, it is very cheap at that price*

ʻandek sâʻa inkelîzi ? = *Have you an English watch ?*
aiwa, ya khawâge, ahe wâḥida ṭayibe = *Yes, sir, here is a good one*
tamanha kâm ? = *How much is it ?*
tamanha arbaʻ ginîye = *Its price is four pounds*
ya sa âm, hiya ghâliya giddan = *Indeed it is very dear*
bi-kam el-ʻêsh (khubz) di l-waqt ? = *How much is bread at present ?*
bi-kam el-laḥmi da ? = *How much is that meat ?*
bi-khamse qurûsh er-raṭl = *Five piastres the pound*
bi-kam ʻalêk sâʻatek ? = *How much did your watch cost you ?*
el-ugre kam ? = *How much is the fare ?*
ed-darage el-awâli wâḥid gineh = *First class one pound*
hena kitâbên, wâḥid, itnên = *Here are two books, one, two*
bi-qaddesh da ? = *How much is that ?*
bi-riyâlên we-nuṣṣ = *Two and a half dollars*
kam el-beled baʻîde min hena ? = *How far is the village from here ?*
hiya mîl tamm min hena = *It is a whole mile from here*
kam sene ʻumrek ? = *How old are you ?*
ʻumri ʻashrîn sena taqrîban = *I am nearly twenty (my age is twenty nearly)*
akhûk kam sene leh ? = *How old is your brother ?*
akhûya luh etnên we-ʻashrîn sene = *My brother is twenty-two*
akhûk eṣ-ṣaghîr kam sene ʻumruh ? = *How old is your little brother ? (Your little brother how many years his age)*
ʻumruh sitt senin = *He is six years old*
tâni yôm el-ʻîd = *The day after the feast*
ana maʻi telâte qurûsh bass = *I have only three piastres with me*

WORD LIST

Broken Plurals of type qutûl

bet, *pl.* buyut = *house*	qalb, *pl.* qulûb = *heart*
ḥaqq, *pl.* ḥuqûq = *claim, right*	qaṣr, *pl.* quṣûr = *palace, castle*
melik, *pl.* mulûk = *king*	

Broken Plurals of type qutal—qital

ôḍa*, *pl.* uwaḍ = *room*	ṣûra*, *pl.* ṣuwar = *picture*

Broken Plurals of type quttâl

ḥâkim, *pl.* ḥukkâm = *governor*	tâgir, *pl.* tuggâr = *merchant*
	ṭâlib, *pl.* ṭullâb = *student*

(For terms expressing "how much?" etc., see above. For coins, weights, etc., see supplementary list, p. 79.)

bass = *only*	rakhîs (*or* rikhîs) = *cheap*
darage = *class*	sena, *pl.* sinîn = *year*
gukh = *cloth*	ugre = *fare*
nasba = *proportion*	'umr = *age*
nuṣṣ = *half*	

EXERCISE

(1) 'andek kutub 'arabi?— aiwa, ya khawâge, 'andena, ahe kutub gedîde = **Have you any Arabic books?—Yes, sir, we have, here are some new books**

(2) el-kitâb da (hal-kitâb) kam tamanuh?—tamanuh 'ashrîn qirsh = **What is the price of this book?—Its price is twenty piastres**

(3) da ghâli ketîr bi-s-si'r da = **It is very dear at that price**

(4) la, hûwa rakhîs qawi bi-s-si'r da = **No, it is very cheap at that price**

(5) bi-qaddesh da?—bi-qirshên = **How much is this?—Two piastres**

(6) bi-kâm ed-dira' min el-gûkh da?—bi-riyâlên = **How much an ell is that cloth?—Two dollars**

(7) ma'kum felûs ?—aiwa, ma'na 'ashrîn qirsh	=	**Have you any money with you ?—Yes, I have twenty piastres**
(8) ya salâm ana ma'i tamâne qurûsh bass	=	**Good heavens, I have only eight piastres with me**
(9) kam sene 'umrek ?—'umri temant 'âsher sene	=	**How old are you ?—I am eighteen**
(10) el-bêt da kebîr qawi, fîh uwaḍ ketîre	=	**That house is very large, there are a great many rooms in it**
(11) mîn er-râgil da ?—hûwa tâgir min et-tuggâr fi l-Iskandarîya	=	**Who is that man ?—he is one of the merchants of Alexandria**
(12) fi l-medîne di buyût ketîre	=	**There are many houses in this city**
(13) el-Qâhira medîne kebîre we-fîha shawâri' leṭîfe	=	**Cairo is a great city and there are beautiful streets in it**
(14) kâm el-ugre ila l-Qâhire ? —ed-darage el-awâle khamsîn qirsh, we-itnên khamse we-'âshrîn	=	**How much is the fare to Cairo ?—First class it is fifty piastres, and second class twenty-five**
(15) tis'a we-telâta kâm ?	=	**How much is nine plus three ?**
(16) khamse min 'ashrîn kâm ?	=	**How much is five from twenty ?**
(17) sab'a fi telâta tâm ?	=	**How much is seven times three ?**
(18) khamse we-'âshrîn 'ala khamse kâm ?	=	**How much is twenty-five divided by five ?**
(19) nasba mîye ila alf ke-nasba khamse ila khamsîn	=	**A hundred is to a thousand as five is to fifty**
(20) ahe maḥaṭṭa, ismiha êy ? —ismiha el-Quṣûr	=	**Here is a station, what is its name ?—Its name is Luxor**

(21) betâ‘ mîn el-qaṣr da ?—huwa qaṣr min el-quṣûr illi li-l-melik = **Who does this palace belong to?—It is one of the palaces of the king**

(22) kâm lek ‘alêh ? li ‘alêh tamâniya wetamânîn qirsh = **How much does he owe you? He owes me eighty-eight piastres**

(23) ‘andi dâr fîha talât biyût we-saṭh = **I have a house with three rooms and a verandah**

(24) akhû khamsîn = **A man of fifty**

(25) qabel sentên = **Two years ago**

(26) awwal waḥde . . . tâni waḥde . . . = **First item . . . second item . . .**

APPENDIX TO LESSON VII

Some of the Commoner Coins and Measures

Coins. (Values must be looked out in current rate of exchange.)

bâra* = *para* (*Syr.*).
qirsh (qurûsh) = *piastre* = 40 *paras*.
faḍḍa = *silver coin, i.e. piastre.*
beshlik (Syria) = *five piastres.*
riyâl (riyâle) (Syr.) = *dollar, usually about* 17–18 *piastres.*
megîdi (Syr.) = 20 *piastres.*
ginîh (giniya) (Eg.) = 5 *dollars*, or 100 *piastres.*
lîra ‘usmanli (Syr.) = *Turkish pound, five megîdi.*

Measures.

qadam = foot.
dera‘ = span.
mîl = mile.

Weights. (Only roughly approximate, subject to local variations.)

miskal	
oqqiye	= 8 miskals.
ruṭl (arṭâl)	= pound, 12 oqqiye.
qantar	= 100 ruṭl.
ṭûlûnâta*	= ton.

Chapter X

THE EIGHTH LESSON—THE GENITIVE

We have seen that a suffixed pronoun attached to a noun denotes the possessive as in bêt-î = " my house ". Instead of that suffix we can add a noun in the same position and similarly convey a possessive meaning, e.g. bêt er-râgil = " the man's house ". Grammarians have observed that there are two kinds of genitive or possessive: (i) the true or logical genitive and (ii) the formal genitive.

(i) The true genitive causes the preceding word to be defined, e.g. kitâb el-walid, " the boy's book " or " the book of the boy ". This specifies a particular book and so defines it as sharply as if the article were prefixed to the " book ". This definition by the following genitive debars us from applying the article to the word so defined, so when we translate into Arabic " the book of the boy " we must be careful not to put " the " before " book " as the following possessive conveys a complete definition and the article would be redundant. So:

kitâb Muḥammad = *The book of Muhammad*

" Muhammad " is defined by its own nature because it is a proper name and so it strictly defines the preceding word, which consequently cannot have the article. And so:—

kitâb abûk = *Thy father's book*

Abûk is defined by the possessive suffix and so defines the preceding " book ". In all these instances of the true genitive the rule is that the first word (the thing or person possessed) may not have the article but still must be regarded as fully defined by the second noun (denoting the possessor or author) which must have its definition either by the article or by its own nature or by a suffixed pronoun.

In Arabic consequently we are unable to express directly " a merchant of the city ", for the following genitive would define the " merchant ", so we are reduced to say " one of the merchants of the city " or " a merchant of the merchants of the city ". In modern colloquial betâ', tabâ', shiyye, or mâl (cf. sect. 14 above) can be inserted and then it is this inserted word which is defined by the possessive and so the preceding noun may or may not have the articles. Thus:—

el-kitâb betâ' er-râgil = *The man's book*
(lit. *the book property of the man*)

No doubt one reason why these words have become so usual in the colloquial is that they enable the uneducated speaker to evade some of the stricter requirements of classical grammar.

These two nouns, the construct (= the thing or person possessed) and the genitive (= the possessor), are bound together in a close connection which the grammarians term " idáfat " (occupation), and two points must be carefully noted about this: (1) the connection is so close that the genitive is treated like a suffix and so the feminine nouns ending in -a (-e) change this to -at (-et) before the genitive just as before a pronominal suffix, and so—

The city of the Prophet = medînet en-nâbî

Remember, therefore, to use -at, -et in such feminines when followed by the genitive. Again, of course, the use of betâ', etc., avoids this. (2) So close is the connection that nothing ought to intervene between the construct and its genitive: usually the qualifying adjective follows the noun it qualifies, but if the genitive follows it has to be postponed so as not to break the connection. So if I want to say " the man's large book " I must express it as " book (of) the man the large " =

kitâb er-râgil el-kebîr. As the kitâb is defined by the following genitive the adjective has to be defined also and this is done by giving it the article. Unfortunately the resultant expression looks to the English reader like " the book of the big man ", but if this had been meant the phrase would have been " (the) book (of) the man and he (is) big ". Again the use of betâ‘, etc., enables us to evade all these requirements.

The Formal Genitive

(ii) The Formal Genitive is that which does not define but merely describes : it does not denote author or possessor but only material, etc. Thus ṣaḥni neḥâs = " a dish of copper ". In this sort of genitive the second (or genitive) word is not necessarily defined—in classical Arabic the second word may be genitive, or accusative, or in apposition with the first ; so with a genitive of this sort either both may have the article, or both may be without, or the second may have it and the first not. It is not possible, however, for the first to have it and the second to be without, nor can we use betâ‘, etc., in this sort of genitive. Thus mesâfit yôm = " a day's distance ", yôm es-safar = " day of departure ", etc.

So the genitive can be used to express material, e.g. bâb khashab = " a door of wood ", which could also be expressed as bâb min khashab = " a door (made) from wood ", or the two words can be treated as in apposition " a door a (piece of) wood " ; in classical Arabic where the cases are shown by distinctive endings it is apparent that the formal genitive of the second, or its apposition with the first, are alternative ways of expressing the material. So sâ‘a dahab, or sâ‘a min dahaq ="a gold watch", etc., laḥm ghanam= "mutton" (i.e. meat of sheep). In these cases both words may take the article, or both may be undefined, thus bâb khashab = " a wooden door ", el-bâb el-khashab = " the wooden door ".

The Formal Genitive Governed by an Adjective

The formal genitive may be governed by an adjective or its equivalent (i.e. the participle of the verb, etc.). Thus :—

ketîr el-mâl = *Great of wealth*
qâlîl el-ʻaql = *Scanty in intelligence*
huwâ faqîr el-ḥâl = *He was of poor condition*
kâtib el-kitâb = *Writer of the book* (=*he who wrote the book*, the katib being a participle equivalent to a verb in sense, to an adjective in form)

Peculiar Use of "Master", "Father", etc., with the Genitive

It is characteristic of all the Semitic languages to use such words as "master", "owner", "father", etc., with abstract (sometimes with other) nouns as descriptives. The words thus used in Arabic are dhû or dû (fem. dhât, dât) "owner", ṣâḥib (fem. ṣaḥibe) "master", ab[1] "father", umm "mother", ibn "son", etc. Thus "father of lies" = "liar".

du ʻilm = *Wise man* (= *owner of wisdom*)
du ʻaql = *Intelligent man*
el-yôm du maṭar = *To-day is rainy* (= *owner of rain*)
du temâm qawâʻid = *An eight-sided figure*
shagare dât zill = *A shady tree*
ṣâḥib ʻadl = *Upright man*
ṣâḥib mâl ketîr = *Very wealthy man*
abû l-faḍl = *Excellent man* (*father of excellence*)
abû shawârib = *Man with long moustaches*
abû guʻrân = *Father of dung* (name of carrion beetle)

[1] Note that ab, akh, ham before the genitive take -û as before a suffix.

umm arba‘ we-arbaîn = *Mother of forty-four* (=centipede)
ibn ‘ashrîn sene = *Man twenty years old*
ibn nâs *or* ibn bêt = *Man of good birth*
ibn âwa = *Jackal*, etc.

All, Every

The words kull, gemî‘ mean "all" or "every"; used with the article they denote "all, the whole", without the article "every".

kull n-nâs, *or* gemî‘ en-nâs = *All men*
en-nâs kulluhum, *or* en-nâs gemî‘hum = *All men*
kull el-medîne, el-medîne kulliha = *All the city*
kull(i) medîne = *Every city*
kull el-yôm, el-yôm kulluh = *All the day, the whole day*
kull(i) yôm = *Every day*
kull(i)na = *All of us*
kull wâḥid = *Every one*

Part

The word ba‘ḍ (ba‘aḍ) denotes "part, some", and is followed by the genitive. Thus :—

ba‘ḍ en-nâs = *Some men*
ba‘ḍ et-tiggâr = *Some merchants*
ba‘ḍina = *Some of us*
ba‘ḍi (ba‘aḍ) min en-nâs = *Some of the men*

Like

Similar in use is misl (mithl) "like", as :—

hûwa misl el-waḥsh = *He is like a wild beast* (= *the like of a wild beast*) hûwa misli = *He is like me* (= *my like*)

In Egyptian dialect zayy, ziyy = "like".

huwa zayyi = *He is like me*

'ala zayy el-hunud = *In the Indian fashion*

Hence ezayy = *what like? how?* ezayyek = *how are you?*

Unlike

Ghêr is used for "other than", "unlike", thus:—

ragil mutemaddin = *A civilized man*

ragil ghêr mutemaddin = *An uncivilized man*

er-ragil ghêr el-mutemaddin = *The uncivilized man*

Thus ghêr becomes a simple negative used before an adjective or its equivalent whose descriptive is denied.

WORD LIST

Plurals of the type aqtâl

nahr	anhâr	= *river*
walad	awlâd	= *child* (this is the literary plural, the vernacular generally prefers wilad)
shagare*	ashgâr	= *tree*
mâl	amwâl	= *property*
ḥâl	aḥwâl	= *state, condition*

Plurals of type qitlân or qutlân

beled	buldân	= *town, country*
fâris	fursân	= *horseman*
ghulâm	ghilmân	= *boy, youth, slave*
shâbb	shubbân	= *young man*

'adad	= *number*	laḥm ghanam	= *mutton, etc.*
ahl	= *family, people*	musâfir (-în)	= *traveller*
akh (ikhwân)	= *brother*	qahwa	= *coffee (beverage)*
bunn	= *coffee (in berry)*	qonṣul	= *consul*
dukkân	= *shop*	sarg	= *saddle*
dukhkhân	= *tobacco*	shêkh	= *old man, chief*
galâle*	= *majesty*	sûq (iswaq)	= *market*
laḥm	= *meat*	wâdi	= *valley*
laḥm baqar	= *beef*	yôm (aiyâm)	= *day*

EXERCISE

(1) kêf ḥâl el-hawa ?—en-nehâr da el-hawa radi	=	**What is the state of the weather ?—To-day the weather is bad**
(2) huwa min wâdi n-Nîl	=	**He is from the Nile valley**
(3) er-rigâl dâk hum min esh-Shâm	=	**Those men are from Damascus**
(4) wên el-kitâb mâli ?—hena el-kitâb mâlek	=	**Where is my book ?—Here is your book**
(5) huwa fi ba'ḍ al-aiyâm fi s-sûq	=	**Some days he is in the market**
(6) zôget el-qonṣul hîya marîḍe giddan	=	**The consul's wife is very ill**
(7) baghl el-musâfir da ma fîsh luh sarg	=	**This traveller's mule has no saddle**
(8) kam 'adad ahl el-Iskanderîya ?	=	**What is the population of Alexandria ?**
(9) betâ' mîn el-qaṣr da ?—da qaṣr Muntaza we-huwa wâhid quṣûr galâlet el-melik	=	**Whose palace is that ?—That is the palace of Muntaza and it is one of the palaces of his majesty the king**
(10) el-gebel da ismuh ey ?—da huwa Gebel Mûsâ	=	**That mountain, what is its name ?—That is Gebel Musa**
(11) min ên el-musâfir ?—huwa el-qonṣul el-faransâwi	=	**Where is that traveller from ?—He is the French consul**
(12) ṣâḥibi fên ?—hûwa fi d-dukkân betâ' et-tâgir	=	**Where is my friend ?—He is in the merchant's shop**
(13) betâ'e min el-gimâl di ?—hîya el-gimâl betâ'et esh-shêkh	=	**Whose are those camels ?—They are the sheikh's**

(14) mîn esh-shêkh ?—esh-shêkh da ismuh Maḥmûd we-huwa kebîr el-beled kullha	=	**Who is the sheikh?—His name is Mahmud and he is the chieftain of all the country**
(15) et-tâgir da hûwa ṣâḥib mâl ketîr	=	**That merchant is very wealthy**
(16) hûwa faqîr el-mâl	=	**He is very poor**
(17) abûya hûwa tâgir we-lâkin hûwa mush ghani	=	**My father was a merchant but he was not wealthy**
(18) ba'ḍ el-musâfirîn hum fi l-Iskanderîya, we-be'duhum fi l-Qâhire	=	**Some of the travellers are in Alexandria and some of them are in Cairo**
(19) en-nâs ba'ḍuhum inkelizîyye we-ba'ḍuhum faransâwiyye	=	**Some of the men are English and some of them French**
(20) ba'ḍina muslimîn we ba'ḍina naṣâra	=	**Some of us are Muslims and some of us are Christians**
(21) wâḥid et-tuggâr hûwa ḥabâshi	=	**One of the merchants is a negro**
(22) ibnek fên ?—ibni huwa fi l-bêt betâ' et-tâgir el-'Agemi	=	**Where is your son?—My son is in the Persian merchant's house**
(23) kull en-nâs hum ikhwân	=	**All men are brothers**
(24) kull wâḥid fi l-mudun di muslim	=	**Every one in these towns is a Muslim**
(25) fi kulli medîne muslimîn	=	**There are Muslims in every town**
(26) 'andek laḥm el-baqar ?—aiwa 'andi	=	**Have you any beef?—Yes, I have**
(27) bi-kam tamanuh ?		**How much is it?**
(28) bi-kâm er-raṭl bunn ?	=	**How much is coffee a pound?**
(29) et-tâgir el-kebîr el-mâl	=	**The very wealthy merchant**

(30) barûdna share 'eḍ-ḍarîb = **Our muskets are the law of the warrior**

(31) ya bint, ya umm el-medalât = **O girl, mother of big earrings**

(32) mâl ma 'endna, mâl ma 'endna = **We have no property, we have no property**
gher el-dagage el-etqaqi **except a cackling hen and a**
we-dêk ma'ha yeqâqi **cock to go with it**
ensûnat ma 'endna ḥeẓûnât **We have no fine women**

(These last three sentences (30–2) are from Bedwin songs given in the *Palestine Exploration Fund's Quarterly Statement* for April, 1925 (pp. 87–8).)

ADDITIONAL EXAMPLES OF THE USE OF THE GENITIVE

bi-smi-llâhi r-raḥmâni r-raḥîm = *In the name of God the merciful, the compassionate*

(Invocation said at the beginning of any undertaking, before partaking of food, etc., and exclamation on seeing the unexpected. As a quotation the classical forms are (usually) preserved, so ism loses its initial *i-* after bi-, as this *i-* is not part of the stem, but *-i* is added after (*i*)*sm*, (A)llah and raḥman as termination of the genitive which follows the preposition, but it is omitted after raḥim because final short vowels are not sounded at the " pause ", i.e., before full stop.)

ya gemel el-bêt = *O camel of the house*

(Women's cry in wailing for the dead master of a house.)

ya shêkh el-'arab = *O sheikh of the Arabs*

(Salutation to the saint Aḥmed el-Bedawi who is buried at Tanta and whose disciples, one of the most popular fraternities of darwishes in Egypt, are known by their wearing red turbans.)

raḥmet allâh 'alêh = *The mercy of God be on him*

(To be said after mentioning by name any person who is dead.)

ṣalât allâh 'alêh we-salâm = *The prayer (= blessing) of God be on him (and peace)*

(Used after every mention of the Prophet. If the speaker does not use this formula a bystander usually says it in a low voice.)

'ala l-'ên we-r-râs, Ya sayyid en-nâs = *On the eyes and head, O lord of men*

(Meaning, I am entirely at your disposal. Note the dual in ên = "eyes", see p. 67 above.)

kulli belad bi-'âdetha = *Every country has its customs*

kulli shayy fi yîd allâh = *Everything is in God's hands*

fi mân allâh (= fi amân . . .) = *In the keeping of God* (= *good-bye*)

salâm hiya ḥatta matla' el-fagr = *It is peace until break of day*

da l-waqt da nuṣṣ en-nehâr = *Already it is midday*

kulli yom arba' marrât = *Four times every day*

fi yôm min ba'ḍ el-aiyâm fi waqt ed-dohr = *On a certain day at noon*

ibn ḥarâm ! = *Rascal !* (= *son of thieves !*)

sitt denânîr dahab = *Six dinars of gold*

(dinar = ancient coin, silver in the lands conquered from the Persians, gold in those taken from the Greeks.)

laḥm ghanam bârid = *Cold mutton*

luqmet 'êsh (khubz) = *A morsel of bread*

kubbâyet môya = *A glass of water*

(These five last are formal or improper genitives.)

kêf ḥâl el-hawa ? = *What is the weather like?* (= *what is the state of the weather?*)

êsh lôm kêfîyetek ? = *How are you* (dial. of Aleppo) ?

(lit. what is the colour of your condition ?)

ma fîsh ḥadde ghêrna fi l-bêt = *There is no one but us in the house*

ya bû naḍḍâre = *O you with spectacles* (bû = abû)

Chapter XI

THE NINTH LESSON—ADJECTIVES OF THE MEASURE AQTAL

The Comparative Degree

The comparative degree of adjectives is formed on the measure of *aqtal,* thus kebîr "great", akbar "greater"; ṣa‘ab "difficult", aṣ‘ab "more difficult"; ṭawîl "long", aṭwal "longer"; ‘ali "high", (= ‘aliy), a‘lâ (= a‘lay) "higher"; ḥarr "hot", aḥarr "hotter", etc. The comparative may be followed by min or an "from" which thus used serves to express "than", and in "western" Arabic ‘ala may be used similarly. Thus :—

aṭwal minnek = *Taller than you*
ash-shams honâk aḥarr minnha hena = *The sun there is hotter than here*

For "better" use aḥsan, but the positive ḥasân = "good" is now used only as a proper name. For "good" use khêr, or ṭayyib.

aḥsan min da ma fîsh = *There is no better than this*

We can also make a comparative by using the word aktar = "more" (from ketîr = "much") and this is the usual method when the adjective contains more than three consonants, thus :—

ana ‘aṭshân aktar minnek = *I am thirstier than you*

(Classical Arabic has a feminine form for the comparative in the measure qutla, e.g. "greater" = *masc.* akbar, *fem.* kubra, but this is no longer used in the colloquial speech.)

The Superlative

The same form is used for the superlative and may then take the article or be otherwise defined, thus el-akbar = "the greatest", el-aṣ‘ab = "the most difficult", etc.

akbar el-kull akbar kulluhum	= *Greatest of all*
akbarhum	= *The greatest of them*
aqṣar eṭ-ṭurûq	= *The shortest way* (= *shortest of the ways*)
aqṣar ṭarîq	= (*The*) *shortest way is* . . .
bi-l-ketîr	= *At most*
bi-l-aktar	= *Generally*

The word kebîr "great" is often used in a superlative sense, as kebîr en-nâs = "greatest of men". Applied to God, akbar serves as superlative, e.g. Allâh akbar = "God is greatest".

Attention should be given to the use of the preposition ‘ala (‘alê-) with an adjective: very often this expresses a quasi-superlative which very nearly corresponds to the English "too", thus:—

el-burnûs betâ‘i hûwa qaṣîr ‘alêk	= *My cloak is too short for you*
el-kitâb da el-inkelîzi huwa ṣa‘ab ‘ala l-walad eṣ-ṣaghîr	= *That English book is too hard for the little boy*

Adjectives Denoting Colour

Adjectives denoting colour have, in the masculine, the same form as comparatives but make their feminine in the measure qatla, thus:—

abyaḍ	*fem.*	bayḍa	= *white*
aswad		sawda (soda)	= *black*
aḥmar		ḥamra	= *red*

azraq	zarqa	= *blue*
aṣfar	ṣafra	= *yellow*
akhdar	khadra	= *green*

Adjectives Denoting Bodily Defects

The same measure is used to denote bodily defects but with the feminine qatlâ. Thus :—

aḥbad	*fem.* ḥadbâ	= *hunch-backed*
akhras	kharsâ	= *dumb*
a'rag	'argâ	= *lame*
a'ma (= a'may)	'amyâ	= *blind*, etc.

ADDITIONAL EXAMPLES OF THE "AQTAL" FORMS

el-'udr aqbah min ed-denb = *The excuse is more shameful than the offence*

ed-darsi da aṣ'ab min et-tâni = *This exercise is harder than the last*

el-yôm ente keslân aktar minnek ems = *To-day you are idler than you were yesterday*

huwa angas min fâret el-ḥabs = *He is more cunning than the prison rat*

ḥaqq el-qawi aqwa = *The right of the stronger is strongest* (= *might is right*)

el-ḥara di aṭwal el-ân mimma saqibân = *This street is longer now than it was formerly*

(mimma = min ma, *than what*)

huwa mush aktar min nuṣṣ mîl = *It is not more than a half mile*

el-bêt d-akbar min dâk = *This house is larger than that*

(d-akbar = da akbar)

huwa akbar minni bi-shahrên = *He is older than I by two months*
huwa akbar bi-ketîr = *He is much older*
aṣfar ʻala akhdar = *Yellowish green*

WORD LIST

ʻâlim = *wise*
ʻâqil = *reasonable, sensible*
baḥr (abḥor) = *sea* (in Egypt also *the Nile*)
dulb = *plane tree*
dunya = *world*
embâriḥ = *yesterday* (Eg.)
ems = *yesterday* (Syr. ʻIraq)
ʻên (ʻeyun) = *eye*
farḥân = *cheerful*
gâhil = *foolish*
gâmiʻ (gawâmeʻ) = *congregational mosque* (i.e. where there is a Friday sermon)
ḥarr = *hot*
khêr = *good, better*
mesgid (mesâgid) = *mosque, oratory* (*not congregational*)
nahr (anhâr) = *river* (*canal* in ʻIraq)
nakhl, -e* = *palm-tree* (*date palm*)
nûr = *light*
qamar (masc.) = *moon*
rîḥ (aryâḥ) = *wind*
shahr (ashhur) = *month*
shedîd = *severe, violent*
ṭarfâ = *tamarisk*
waraq = *paper*
zahra* (ezhâr) = *flower*

EXERCISE

(1) ente akbar minni = **You are older than I am**
(2) eṭ-ṭarîq da huwa aṭwal min eṭ-ṭarîq et-tâni = **This road is longer than the other one**
(3) ed-darsi da (had-dars) asʻab ʻalêya = **This lesson is too hard for me**
(4) en-nakhle di hiya aʻla min dârna = **This palm-tree is higher than our house**
(5) ma fîsh nahr aṭwal fi d-dunya kullha min baḥr en-Nîl el-mubârek = **In all the world there is no river longer than the blessed Nile**

(6) eṭ-ṭarfâ di aḥsan min ed-dulb = **This tamarisk is more beautiful than the plane-tree**

(7) al-'âlim aḥsan min el-gâhil = **The wise man is better than the fool**

(8) huwa akbar minnek, ente a'lan minnuh = **He is older than you, you are taller than he**

(9) er-rigâl dôl 'aṭshânîn akbar minni = **Those men are thirstier than I**

(10) fi l'baḥr el-akhmar el-hawa aḥarr minnuh hêna = **In the Red Sea the weather is hotter than here**

(11) el-gimâl hîye aqwa min el-ḥamîr = **Camels are stronger than asses**

(12) esh-shagare hiye khadre we-ezhârha ṣafra = **The tree is green and its flowers are yellow**

(13) el-mara di hiye 'amye = **This woman is blind**

(14) el-yôm ente keslân ketîr, aktar minnek embâriḥ = **To-day you are very lazy, more than you were yesterday**

(15) el-yôm abrad min ems = **To-day is colder than yesterday**

(16) akhûk en-nehâr da aḥsan = **Is your brother better to-day?**

(17) ghulâm aqil kher min shêkh gâhil = **A sensible youth is better than a foolish old man**

(18) el-khawâge Maḥmûd fên? = **Where is Mr. Mahmûd?**

(19) huwa fi l-gâmi' el-akbar = **He is in the principal mosque**

(20) nûr esh-shems aktar min nûr el-qamar = **The light of the sun is stronger than the light of the moon**

(21) huwa akbar minnek bi-shahrên = **He is older than you by two months**

(22) el-yôm er-rîḥ ashadd bi-ketîr minnuh ems	= **To-day the wind is much stronger than yesterday**
(23) el-'abd el-aswad huwa 'abduh	= **The black slave is his**
(24) el-baḥr huwa azraq	= **The sea is blue**
(25) huwa min el-bahr el-akhmar	= **He is from the Red Sea**
(26) 'ênha hiye sôda	= **Her eye is black**
(27) el-waraq huwa abyaḍ	= **The paper is white**
(28) el-waraq da huwa abyaḍ, mush kida ?	= **This paper is white, is it not so ?**
(29) el-bêt d-akbar min da	= **This house is larger than that**
(30) el-'agûze di hiye faqîre ketîr we-'amya	= **This woman is very poor and blind**
(31) el-bint es-sôda farhâne qawi	= **The black girl is very cheerful**
(32) di aḥsan lokânda fi beledek ?	= **Is this the best hotel in your town ?**
(33) ente akbar qader	= **Your position be greater**

(Apology for some impropriety in speech.)

CHAPTER XII

THE TENTH LESSON—THE VERB, PERFECT TENSE, REGULAR FORM

GENERAL IDEA OF THE VERB

THE Semitic verb is built up from a root which normally consists of three consonants which make a kind of skeleton around and in which the verb stem is formed. The "irregular", or more properly the "defective" verbs, are simply those in which one or other of the root consonants is a weak letter such as w or y which is absorbed by a neighbouring vowel, the resultant modifications following clear phonetic principles.

TENSES

The verb has three "tenses" so-called, but these are not quite "tenses" in the European sense. These are generally known as (i) the Perfect, (ii) the Imperfect, and (iii) the Imperative. The Imperative is, of course, the form used for command, the Perfect most often refers to the past, but not necessarily so, and the Imperfect to the present or future. In reality the time of the sentence is expressed by means of an adverb, or particle, just as in English we may say "I go" in the present, and also "I go there to-morrow", using the same tense for future time.

THE PERFECT TENSE

In the Perfect of the Primary form of the verb the three consonants of the root are vocalized by two vowels inserted between the two pairs of consonants: the second of these may be -a-, -i-, or -u-; the first is properly an obscure -a-. Generally the -i- or -u- occurs in the second place when the verb expresses a state not an action, and most often -u- if the state is a lasting one, -i- if it is merely temporary. Thus, action qatal = " kill " with -a- in the second place, temporary state ghadib = " be angry ", permanent state ḥasun = " be beautiful ". There is, however, a tendency, especially in Egypt and Syria, to make the first vowel assimilate to the second and so we get birid = " be cold " (for barid), tilim = " be blunt " (for talim), suqut = " fall " (for saqut), sughur = " be small " (for saghur), kusul = " be lazy " (for kasul), etc. In all cases it will be remembered that the first vowel was originally -a- and, when one of the " throat " sounds (h, ', gh, etc.) is next this, -a- is preserved, otherwise it generally weakens to -e- or -i- in the usual way. In every case the -a- sound is held to be correct but it sounds a little pedantic and is not colloquial unless a " throat " consonant comes next.

The persons of the tense are formed by adding pronominal forms to the stem produced by vocalizing the root. Thus:—

Sing.	1.		ḍarábt (*ḍarábet)	= *I beat*
	2.	masc.	ḍarábt (*ḍarábet)	= *thou didst beat*
		fem.	ḍarábti	= *thou* (fem.) *didst beat*
	3.	masc.	ḍárab	= *he beat*
		fem.	ḍárabet, ḍárabit	= *she beat*
Plur.	1.		ḍarábna	= *we beat*
	2.		ḍarábtu	= *you beat*
	3.		ḍárabu	= *they beat*

The forms marked (*) are characteristic of 'Iraq, especially when the next word begins with a consonant. In Egypt and Syria it is more usual in such case to add -i to prevent three consonants coming together, as:—

ḥafaẓt-i taqriban talat awgoh = *I have learned nearly three pages*

where the verb ḥafaẓt (sing. 1st) has -i thus added.

Exactly the same terminations are used with verbs containing -i-, or -u-, and those in which both vowels are -i-i- and -u-u- by assimilation, but in Syria (chiefly) the vernacular often loses an unaccented -i- or -u-, thus in the 3rd fem. sing. the verb sharibit = "she has drunk", commonly becomes shiribit in Egypt and Syria, and Syrian then permits shirbit, and in the 3rd plur. shirbu. Some other dialects tend to leave out the unaccented short vowel when it comes before an accented syllable, e.g. in Oman ktebt = ketebet = "I wrote", etc., where the vowel between the k and t is really a very short half vowel. These contractions form the most characteristic features of the different dialects, and, as they are all symptoms of general tendencies, the learning of a new dialect when one is known is no great difficulty, least so when the parent form and basal system is understood.

The following summary of the Perfect terminations will be found convenient :—

	Singular		*Plural*
	masc.	*fem.*	
1.	-t (-et)		-na
2.	-t (-et)	-ti	-tu
3.	—	-et, -it	-u

The Verb with Suffixes

The pronominal suffixes already given (p. 40) can be added to the verb and then denote the object. The -i of the 1st sing. when added to the verb has a "supporting" N inserted and so becomes -n-i.

Thus	ḍarab	= *he beat*
	ḍarabni	= *he beat me*
	ḍarabek	= *he beat thee*, etc.
so	ḍarabna	= *we beat*
	ḍarabnâk	= *we beat thee*
	ḍarabnâh	= *we beat him*
	ḍarabnâha	= *we beat her*, etc.
and	ḍarabt	= *I beat*
	ḍarabtek	= *I beat thee*
	ḍarabtiha	= *I beat her*
	ḍarabtuhum	= *I beat them* (-u- inserted by assimilation to following -u-)

It will be noticed that in such a form as ḍarabnâk there are three elements (1) verb ḍarab, (2) subject -nâ, and (3) object -k, and this order is the classical model for the verbal sentence, although colloquial speech commonly permits the subject to come before the verb as in English, provided of course the subject is a noun substantive ; but the subject after the verb is more strictly correct. In general summary the arrangement of the sentence is :—

(*a*) Verb—Subject—Object : normal order.

(*b*) Subject—Verb—Object : permitted in colloquial.

(*c*) Verb—Object—Subject : necessary when the subject is "restricted" by the use of illa = "only, except", as ma ḍarabshi Muhammad illa ana = "no one beat Muhammad but only I".

(*d*) Object—Subject—Verb : interrogative, as êy râgil ḍarabt ? = "which man did you beat ?"

The Negative Verb

The verb is made negative by ma ('Iraq mu) before it, and colloquial speech commonly adds -sh (-shi), thus :—

ma ḍarabtish = *I did not beat*
ma ḍarabtish = *thou didst not beat*
ma ḍarabsh = *he did not beat*
ma ḍarabetsh = *she did not beat*
ma ḍarabnash = *we did not beat*
ma ḍarabtush = *you did not beat*
ma ḍarabush = *they did not beat*

The -i- is inserted when three consonants come together and it is permissible to add -i after -sh when it is preceded by a consonant and the next word begins with a consonant thus bringing three consonants into contact.

The negative can be added after the suffix has been attached as ma ḍarabtuhsh = "I have not beaten him".

The Interrogative Verb

A verb sentence in the interrogative may be so simply by the tone in which it is spoken, or -sh (-shi) may be added to the verb, as ḍarabnash = "did we beat?", ḍarabtish = "didst thou beat?", etc.

Another form of interrogative is produced by using ya'ni, thus ya'ni kharagu 'alêh? = "did they rebel against him?"

Note on the Uses of the Persons

The first, second, or third person of the verb must be used according to the person of the subject: if the subject is feminine singular or a broken plural the 3rd fem. singular should be used. When the nominative does not follow after the verb the verb must be put in the plural with a plural subject but if the subject is definitely expressed and follows the verb it is optional whether the verb is in the plural or singular.

WORD LIST

(i) *Verbs*

(The vowels in brackets denote those required in the imperfect.)

'amal	(a)	= *do*
dakhel	(u)	= *enter*
ḍarab	(a)	= *strike*
fahim	(a)	= *understand*
ḥafaẓ	(a)	= *learn by heart*
ḥaṣal	(u)	= *happen*
keteb	(u)	= *write*
khaliṣ	(u)	= *finish*
kharag	(u)	= *go out*
misik	(u, i)	= *seize*
nizil	(i)	= *go down*
qa'ad	(u)	= *sit*
raga'	(i)	= *return*
sami'	(a)	= *hear*
shirib	(a)	= *drink*
shirib dukhkhan		= *smoke*
ṣaraf	(i)	= *dismiss, waste*
ṭalab	(u)	= *seek*
ṭala'	(u)	= *rise (sun) go up*

(ii) *Nouns*

'askari	= *soldier*
'inab	= *grapes*
karm	= *vine, vineyard*
maḥaṭṭa	= *railway station*
mektûb (mekâtîb)	= *letter*
qalam	= *pen*
ṣabaḥ	= *morning*
saroq	= *thief*
ṣêd	= *hunting, fishing*
teskeri	= *ticket*
wagh (awgoh)	= *page*

(iii) *Particles and Nouns used as particles*

amâm	= *before, in presence of*
dilwaqt	= *now, at once*
emta	= *when*
fe-	= *and, and so*
lamma	= *when*
qabl	= *before*
qabl ma	= *before that . . .*
taqriban	= *nearly*

EXERCISE

(1) kharag dilwaqt	= **He has just gone out**
(2) ya walad, êsh 'amalt ?—ḥafaẓti talât awgoh taqribân	= **Boy, what have you done ?—I have learned nearly three pages by heart**
(3) ṭala'et esh-shems	= **The sun has risen** (sun fem.)
(4) ḥaṣal ḥaṣal	= **It certainly happened**
(5) ketebt bi-qalam	= **I wrote with a pen**
(6) nizil min 'ala gemel	= **He dismounted from a camel**
(7) nizilt li-karm el-'inab	= **I went down the vineyard**
(8) ma da 'amalti eṣ-ṣabâḥ da, ya bint ?—ana katebt gawâb	= **What have you done this morning, girl ?—I wrote a letter**

(9) ente qa'edte kâm yôm fi Miṣr ?—qa'edt arb'a yôm = **How long did you stay in Cairo ?—I stayed four days**

(10) nizilt ila l-maḥatta we-ṭelebte teskari = **I went down to the station and asked for a ticket**

(11) sami'û we-lâkin ma fahimûsh = **They heard but did not understand**

(12) ma semi'nash 'annuh = **We have heard nothing about him**

(13) ṭelebtûna n-nehâr da ?—la, ma ṭelebnâkumsh = **Have you been looking for us to-day ?—No, we have not been looking for you**

(14) er-râgil misikni min îdu = **The man seized me with his hand**

(15) entu qa'edtu fên ? = **Where are you staying ?**

(16) fahimtush entu kelâmi ? = **Do you understand what I said ?**

(17) aiwa, eḥna (-ḥna) fahimnâh = **Yes, we understand**

(18) ḍarabtesh khaddâmi ?—la, ma ḍarabtesh khaddâmek = **Did you strike my servant ?—No, I did not strike your servant**

(19) ḍarabkum el-'askari ?—ya'ni ḍarabek el-'askari ? = **Did the soldier strike you ?—Did the soldier strike thee ?**

(20) emta raga'te min eṣ-ṣêd ?—raga'te sâ'atên = **When did you come back from hunting ?—I came back at two o'clock**

(21) esh ṭalab ?—ma fahimtish êsh ṭalab = **What was he looking for ?—I do not know what he was looking for**

(22) fên el-gawâb elli ibnek ketebtuh ? = **Where is the letter your son wrote ?**

(23) ṭelebt mîn ente ?—ana ṭelebt el-khawâge Maḥmûd	= **Who were you looking for? —I was looking for Mr. Mahmud**
(24) mîn ḍarab el-walad eṣ-ṣaghîr ?	= **Who beat the little boy?**
(25) min ên kharagt ?	= **Where did you come out from?**
(26) wâḥid Rûmi nizil min el-Quds ila Jâfâ	= **A Greek went down from Jerusalem to Jaffa**
(27) fi tâni yôm kharag.	= **The next day he went off**
(28) lamma khaliṣ re-kharag	= **When he had finished he went out**
(29) fulân ḥaḍir amâm el-qâdi	= **So and so appeared before the judge**
(30) min qable sikin fi dâri	= **Formerly he lived in my house**
(31) es-sâraq dakhel fi l-lêl fi dâr el-khubbâz	= **The thief entered by night into the baker's house**
(32) nefed es-sahm we-l-ḥamdu li-llâh ḥaṣal khêr 'ala kede	= **The arrow has passed and the praise of God has prevailed beyond that of this person**

(Some words in praise of a person or created thing have been uttered and all present fear their blighting effect until some passing accident has befallen the person or thing praised or some words have been uttered which have transferred the praise from the creature to the Creator, then the dreaded omen is averted, " the arrow has passed . . .")

Chapter XIII

THE ELEVENTH LESSON—THE IMPERFECT TENSE OF THE REGULAR VERB

The Form of the Imperfect

The Imperfect has the same three consonants as the Perfect, but only one vowel is inserted and this is placed between the last two consonants, the first consonant being vocalised by the help of the prefix which denotes the person. In the 2nd fem. sing. and in the 2nd–3rd plural a suffix is added also. The inserted vowel may be -a- (-o-), -i-, or -u-, and that vowel is not always the same in the different dialects: this can only be learned from the dictionary. In the case of the verb ḍ-r-b = " beat " the inserted vowel is -a-, thus -ḍrab, and the tense is then formed as follows:—

Singular.	1.		áḍrab	= *I beat*
	2.	masc.	tíḍrab	= *thou beatest*
		fem.	tíḍrabi	= *thou* (fem.) *beatest*
	3.	masc.	yíḍrab	= *he beats*
		fem.	tíḍrab	= *she beats*
Plural.	1.		níḍrab	= *we beat*
	2.		tíḍrabu	= *you beat*
	3.		yíḍrabu	= *they beat*

The same prefixes and suffixes are used when the vowel stem has -u- or -i-, as askun = " I dwell ", tiskun = " thou dwellest ", etc., aktib = " I write ", tiktib = " thou writest ", etc. We have given the prefixes above with vowel -i-, except in the 1st sing., thus ti-, yi-, ni-: but this is the " obscure "

4*

vowel (originally -a-) and may sometimes sound as -e-, sometimes as -a-, this last usually before a "throat" sound such as ḥ, ', gh, etc.; in Egypt it often happens that the vowel of the prefix is modified to agree with the vowel of the stem so that yiskut "he is silent" becomes yuskut, etc. In 'Iraq, on the other hand, the prefix more often has -a-, especially when the following consonant is emphatic, thus taḍrab, yaḍrab, etc., for tiḍrab, yiḍrab. In Egypt one may hear both ya'rif and yi'rif "he knows". The accent given above is true for Syria, but in Egypt it is carried forward when there is a suffix, so that we get tiḍrábi, tiḍrábu, yiḍrábu; in 'Iraq it is still further carried forward when there is a suffix, and so we get taḍrabí, taḍrabú, yaḍrabú.

Summary

The following summary shows the Imperfect formatives in general:—

	Singular.		*Plural.*
	masc.	*fem.*	
1.	a--	a--	ni--
2.	ti--	ti--i	ti--u
3.	yi--	ti--	yi--u

Prefixed bi-, be-

The modern colloquial of Egypt and Syria often prefixes the syllable be-, bi- (from badd = "remove", whence colloquial baddi = "I want to . . ."). With a- this makes ba-, with yi- it makes bi-, otherwise it is prefixed to the personal formative. Thus:—

badrab = *I beat*
betiḍrab = *thou beatest*
betiḍrabi = *thou* (fem.) *beatest*

bidrab = *he beats*
betidrab = *she beats*
benidrab = *we beat*
betidrabu = *you beat*
bidrabu = *they beat*

But sometimes beyidrab(u) may be heard for bidrab(u): when the first vowel is -u- we do not of course get contraction in the 3rd masc., thus in Egyptian with yuskum "dwell" for yiskun we get beyuskum (not biskun), etc. It will be understood that the whole formation is a vulgarism and avoided in formal speech and in converse with the educated. Finally the b- sometimes becomes m- before n- and so we have menidrab "we beat" for benidrab, menuskun "we dwell" for benuskum (= beniskun), etc.

Thus: talet wahde bisbogh daqno u-shawarbo = "third item, he dyes his beard and moustaches" (Malinjoud: *Textes en dialecte de Damas* in *J. Asiat.* (1924), p. 271). This is a specimen of the speech of an illiterative native of Damascus, note the use of u- "and" for we-.

The Imperfect with Suffixes

The Imperfect takes the suffixes in the same way as the Perfect, thus yetlub or yitlub (Eg. yutlub) "he seeks", yitlubni = "he seeks me", yitlubna = "he seeks us", tetlub = "she seeks", tetlubni = "she seeks me", tetlubek = "she seeks thee", tetlubha = "she seeks her", tetlubhum = "she seeks them", yitlubu = "they seek", yitlubûni = "they seek me", yitlubûkun = "they seek you", etc.

The Interrogative and Negative

The Interrogative and Negative are formed with the same additions as in the perfect: adrabsh = "do I beat?" tidrabsh = "dost thou beat?" etc.; negative ma adrabsh =

"I do not beat", ma tiḍrabsh = "thou dost not beat", ma yidrabsh = "he does not beat", always allowing the addition of -i before a consonant to prevent three consonants in succession: so colloquial ma biḍrabsh, ma betiḍrabsh, etc., and with the suffixes ma tiḍrabnish, ma yiḍrabush, ma tiḍrabuhash, etc.

Principal and Subordinate Verbs

The subordinate verb can follow the principal verb in Arabic and have its proper person and tense. Thus the English "I am able to beat" = "I am able (that) I beat" = aqdar aḍrab; there is no need to express the "to" or "that" of English, but simply to render the two verbs in the same person, in this case in the 1st sing. So "he is not able to write" = ma yeqdarsh yektub ("he is not able he writes"), etc.

Imperfect Modified to Express the Present

Modern colloquial speech introduces ʻammâl before the imperfect to give the sense of the present, the ʻammâl becoming feminine ʻammâle*, or plural ʻammâlîn where necessary to agree with the agent. Thus, ana ʻammâl aktub = "I am writing", ente ʻammâl tektub = "thou art writing", hîya ʻammâle tektub = "she is writing", hum ʻammâlîn yektub = "they are writing". It is permissible to add the be- as well, thus ente ʻammâl betektub, etc. This is a somewhat clumsy way of expressing the present, though in common use; a much simpler method is to use the active participle as in ana kâtib = "I am writing".

Imperfect Modified to Express the Future

There are several ways employed in modern colloquial to express the future:—

(i) The particle bidd with the suffixed pronoun may be placed before the imperfect, thus ente biddek tergi‘ = “thou wilt return”, huwa bidduh yergi‘ = “he will return”, eḥna biddina nergi‘ = “we will return”, etc.

(ii) The participle mâshi (= “walking”), fem. mâshiye*, plural mâshiyîn, may be added before the imperfect, thus êsh mâshi te‘mal? = “what are you going to do?” hîye mâshiye tektub = “she is going to write”, entu mâshiyîn tektubu = “you are going to write”, etc.

(iii) The participle râyiḥ, fem. râyiḥe*, plur. rayiḥin meaning “going” can be used in a similar way, thus ana râyiḥ aḍrab = “I am going to beat”, ente râyiḥ tektub = “thou art going to write”, etc.

Mâshi is the participle of a verb with weak final (cf. p. 149 below) and râyiḥ of one with a weak medial (cf. p. 138 below).

Note on the Imperfect

It must be carefully noted that the a- of the 1st person singular is a fixed personal prefix which does not modify; in the other persons the vowel may sound -i-, -e-, or -a-, as ti-, te-, ta-, etc., according to dialect, but -a- is *generally* (and should be always) before a “throat” letter, whilst it is common (especially in Egypt) to assimilate before stem vowel -u-, thus yuskut (also yiskut), ya‘raf (rarer yi‘raf), etc.

WORD LIST

Verbs

‘arif	(i)	= *know*	lazim		= *be obliged*
ḥeḍer	(a)	= *be present*	naqaṣ	(a)	= *reduce*
ḥasab	(u)	= *reckon*	qadar	(i)	= *be able, can*
kasar	(a)	= *break*	sa’al	(a)	= *ask (question)*

Other words

'ala shân, 'ashân	= *because*; 'ala shân êy ?= *why ?* (Egypt)	in	= *that*
ba'îd	= *far away, remote*	lezûm	= *necessity*
fôq	= *above*	saḥn (suḥûn)	= *plate*
fulân	= *so and so*; el-khawage fulan =*Mr. N.*	sikka	= *road*; sikket el-hadîd=*railway* (*lit. chemin de fer*)
ghurûb	= *setting* (*of the sun*)	ṭebeqa	= *apartment, flat* (*in a house*)
ḥisâb	= *reckoning, bill, account*	ṭalg	= *snow*
		ẓâbiṭ	= *officer*

EXERCISE

(1) tiṭlub min ente ?—ana aṭlub el-khawâge Aḥmed, yeskun fên ? = **Who are you looking for ?—I am looking for Mr. Ahmed. Where does he live ?**

(2) huwa yuskum fi shâri'a l-Madebegh = **He lives in Madebegh Street**

(3) ma a'rifshi fên yeskun = **I do not know where he lives**

(4) yinzil ṭalg = **Snow is falling**

(5) nirgi' fi s-sikka di ? = **Shall we come back this way ?**

(6) emta tirgi'u min eṣ-ṣêd ?—nergi' ba'd ghurûb esh-shems = **When will you return from hunting ? — We shall return after sunset**

(7) eẓ-ẓâbiṭ da yuskun fên ?—huwa yuskun fi ṭ-ṭebeqa illi fôq eṭ-ṭebeqa illi askun fîh = **Where does the officer live ?—He lives in the flat above mine**

(8) ta'rif el-khawâge (fulân) ?—a'rifuh ḥaqq el-ma'rifa.—yuskun fên ?—yuskun fi l-Khurunfîsh.—huwa ba'îd = **Do you know Mr. N. ?—I know him very well indeed.—Where does he live ?—He lives in the Khurunfish.**

min hêna ?—huwa mush aktar min wâḥid mîl	—Is that far from here ?—Not more than a mile
(9) bituskun fên ?—baskun fi wasṭ el-medîne	= Where do you live ?—I live in the middle of the city
(10) ma aqdirsh asma'	= I cannot hear
(11) bete'rifuhsh ?	= Do you know him ?
(12) êsh el-kalâm da, teḥsubni gâhil bi-kull shayy (ḥage) ?	= What is that statement ?—Do you suppose that I am altogether an idiot ?
(13) ma a'rifshe wâḥid bi-l-ism da	= I do not know anyone of that name
(14) êsh te'mal ?—aktub gawâb	= What are you doing ?—I am writing a letter
(15) beteshrabshi qahwe ?	= Will you drink some coffee ?
(16) êsh ente 'ammâl bete'mal ? —ana 'ammâl baktub ba'ḍ mekâtîb	= What are you doing ?—I am writing some letters
(17) teqdir tefham el-kitâb da ? la ma aqdirsh afhamuh 'alishân huwa ṣa'ab ketîr	= Can you understand that book ?—No, I cannot understand it because it is too difficult
(18) yeqdir yeḥsub el-ḥisâb da ? —fi fikri ma yeqdirsh yeḥsubuh	= Can he reckon that account ? —I think he cannot
(19) êsh biṭlub ?—ma a'rifsh êsh biṭlub	= What is she looking for ?—I do not know what she is looking for
(20) betes'al 'an êy ?	= What are you inquiring about ?
(21) teqdirsh teḥḍar ente ?	= Can you be ready ?
(22) 'alishân êy te'mel kida ? —ma a'rifsh	= Why is she acting like that ? —I do not know
(23) ḥaqq 'alêk in te'mal kida	= It is necessary for you to do so

(24) ma yelzim an te'mal da	= It is not necessary for you to do that
(25) ma lêksh lezûm tes'aluh	= You have no need to ask him
(26) we-ba'd yômên kharag	= And after two days he went away
(27) el-môya kulle yôm betin-qaṣ	= The water gets less every day
(28) ana lazamtek leinnek tefḍal hena	= I charge you to remain here
(29) ti'rif tiktub bi-l-'arabi ?	= Can you write Arabic ?
(30) ma a'rifsh el-qirâye faḍlan 'an el-kitâbe	= I cannot read, much less write

CHAPTER XIV

THE TWELFTH LESSON—THE IMPERATIVE, THE PARTICIPLES, THE PASSIVE

(a) THE IMPERATIVE: FORM

THE Imperative uses the same stem as the Imperfect, has the same suffixes, but does not employ the personal prefixes. When the stem begins with a consonant which is followed immediately by a vowel this can be pronounced without trouble, and this, as we shall see later (cf. p. 124 below), actually is the case with verbs whose roots have a weak consonant such as w or y as their second radical. In the ordinary three consonant verbs, however, this gives a group of two consonants at the beginning, e.g. ḍrab "strike", which as it stands cannot be pronounced. Ordinarily, therefore, a vowel is prefixed and this vowel is i-, thus iḍrab "strike", etc., but when the vowel in the stem is -u- this prefixed vowel assimilates to it and so we get urqud "lie down" (also irqud). In Syrian dialect we often find a very short inserted vowel (half-vowel) instead of the prefixed, thus sherab (sh'rab) "drink" for ishrab, mesik (m'sik) "seize" for imsik, etc. This vowel, whether prefixed or inserted, has no bearing upon the meaning and is merely a phonetic addition to enable the initial group of consonants to be pronounced. The imperfect-imperative stem thus vocalised expresses the command given in the masculine singular, i.e. to one man, addressed to a woman the termination -i is added, and to more than one person the plural ending -u.

Thus we get the Imperative system :—

Singular	*masc.*	iḍrab = *beat*
	fem.	iḍrabi
Plural		iḍrabu

Imperative with suffixes.

The imperative may take the same suffixes as the perfect and imperfect, provided the sense of the verb allows a direct object, thus iḍrabuh = " beat him ", irsalûni = " do you (pl.) send me ", etc.

(*b*) The Imperative : Use

The imperative expresses the direct command, thus :—

uskut	= *Be silent*
ighsil yêdêk we-wishshek	= *Wash your hands and face*
infah el-ḥammâl	= *Call for the porter*
ya sâyis, ighsil ḥiṣâni	= *Groom, wash my horse*
ya walad, inzil ila l-bustân	= *Boy, go down to the garden*
ya bint, irgi'i	= *Girl, go back*
irsalû wilâdkum ila l-medrese	= *Send your children to the school*
ya bint, uqfuli l-bâb	= *Girl, shut the door*
ighsilu ayâdikum	= *Wash your hands*
idkhul, ya 'ammi	= *Come in, my uncle*

Sometimes the command is expressed by the imperfect and not by the imperative. Thus :—

(i) In Arabic, as in all the Semitic languages, the imperative may not be used in the negative, but the imperfect must be employed in its place, thus for " do not beat him " we must say ma tiḍrabuhsh. Always the Semitic languages insist on " thou shalt not steal ", not " do not steal ". So :—

ya walad, ma tesraqsh = *Boy, do not steal*
ma tis'alsh = *Do not ask*
ma teḍrab el-kelb dîk = *Do not beat that dog*
ma teshrab min el-môya da = *Do not drink of this water*

(ii) Out of politeness the imperfect may be substituted for the imperative, as—

tek tub gawâb li = *Write me a letter*
teṭla fôq, min faḍlek = *Please go up above*

(iii) After ma = " but " it is necessary to substitute the imperfect for the imperative, thus—

ma teshrab dukhkhân, min faḍlek = *But please smoke*

(iv) Usually the imperfect is used in commands with ya . . . ya . . . = " either . . . or . . . ", as—

ya teq'ud ya tekhrug = *Either sit down or go out*
ya teskut ya teṣduq = *Either be silent or speak the truth*

(v) After the (pleonastic) imperative of baqa, i.e. *sing. masc.* ibqa, *fem.* ibqi, *plur.* ibqu, meaning " be, continue ", the imperfect is used as the imperative is already expressed by ibqa, etc. So—

ibqa tergi' ḥâlan = *Return shortly*
ibqu teṣduqu = *Speak the truth*

But here it is also possible to use the baqa in the imperfect, as

tibqa tesallim li 'ala abûk = *Pray remember me to your father*
tibqu tefaḍḍal = *Please sit down*

(vi) The imperative has only the second person as this alone can be employed in a direct command. An indirect command or jussive in the first or third person necessarily uses the imperfect, thus :—

argi' = *Let me turn back*
ma yergi'sh = *Let him not turn back*
nekhrug min el-bêt = *Let us go out of the house*
Allâh ma yiḥrimnâsh wilâdna = *May God not bereave us of our children*

Thus commands sometimes find expression as imperatives, sometimes as imperfects. But it is also possible to use nouns for command as in English where " silence " means " be silent ". Arabic grammarians regard all words of command which cannot receive the feminine -i or plural -u as nouns and amongst these include the cries made in driving animals, etc. Other commands again assume a verb which is implied but not expressed, as andek = " with thee ", meaning " halt ", and ala mahlekum = " at your leisure ", meaning " (go) more slowly ".

ta'âla = *come*
hât = *give* (*me*)
yalla = *go quickly*
mashi = *go quickly* (imperat. of mashi = *walk*)
'ala mahlekum = *go slowly*
oṣbur = *stop*
'andek (-kum) = *halt*
waqqif = *stop*

(*c*) The Active Participle : Form

The active participle has the form *singular masculine* qâtil, *fem.* qâtile, *plural* qâtilîn. Properly it is a noun (adjective) and all we have said about the use of the noun in sentences applies here. Thus :—

huwa sâkin fên ? = *Where is he living ?*
hiye sâkine fên ? = *Where is she living ?*
hum gâlisîn fên ? = *Where are they staying ?*

(*d*) Active Participle: Use

The active participle is used as equivalent to the present tense, but as the participle is a noun the sentence in which it occurs without a verb is void of time sense and is merely descriptive, though colloquial usage assumes a present time. Thus :—

ana kâtib = *I am writing*

When a verb is used the participle belongs to the same time as the verb, thus using kân = " he was ".

kân gâlis ma'uh we-ḥaḍaru wâḥid 'aiyân = *He was sitting with him and they brought to him a certain sick person*

As the participle is a noun adjective it is descriptive of the accompanying or implied substantive and not (as may be the case in English) of the circumstances in which the action of the verb takes place, thus " having closed the door I went away " must be " after I had closed the door I went away " = ba'd ma qafalt el-bâb kharaget; " knowing that it was raining I did not go out " becomes " because I knew it was raining I did not go out " = mâdâm 'irift inn nizil maṭar ma kharagetsh.

But it may be used to describe the agent or object at the time of the verb's action, as—

qa'adet shârib = *I sat drinking*
ana dâkhil shuftuh = *I saw him as I was going out*
ana shuftuh dâkhil = *I saw him going out*

This is especially the case when the description is introduced as a kind of parenthesis by means of we-, thus :—

wâḥid nadahna we-ḥna mâshiyîn fi sh-shâri' (we-ḥna = we-eḥna) = *A certain man called to us, and we were walking in the street*

(*e*) The Passive Participle : Form

The passive participle has the form mektûb (maktûb) with fem. -e*, plural -în.

(*f*) Passive Participle : Use

The passive participle describes a condition already made effective and so not contemporary with the action of the verb, e.g. :—

wagadtuh maqtûl = *I found him* (*already*) *killed*

qatalûh el-magrûḥ = *They killed him who had been wounded*

It is not possible to use the passive participle in such as "I saw the man being beaten", we must say "I saw the man, they were beating him" = shuft er-râgil yeḍrabûh.

(*g*) The Passive Voice

(i) Some verbs are quasi-passive, i.e. verbs of state conveying a sense equivalent to a passive, thus tilif = "perish" (talaf = "destroy"), sikin = "be inhabited" (sakan = "inhabit"), fiqir = "become poor" (faqar = "be poor"), niqiṣ, nuquṣ = "be diminished", etc.

(ii) Derived forms in t- (really reflexive) often convey a passive sense (on these verbs see p. 125 below).

(iii) Very often the third person plural is used where we should employ the passive, thus "it is said" is rendered "they say", etc.

(iv) The passive participle is the one passive form which admits of free use as conveying a passive sense, thus :—

mektûb = *It is written* (i.e. *it is God's decree,* reply to a beggar who shows deformities with the intention of exciting compassion).

When a verb is transferred from the active to the passive the logical object becomes the new (formal) agent, thus "he beat the boy" becomes "the boy was beaten": the original agent may then sometimes be expressed by the help of the preposition min = "by", e.g. "the man beat the boy" = "the boy was beaten by the man", but this is unpleasing in Arabic and so unusual that it is not easily understood, so that when the true agent is expressed it is strongly preferable to use the active; thus to translate "the boy was beaten by the man" say "the boy was beaten, the man beat him" = el-walad meḍrub ḍarabuh er-râgil; or better still transfer the whole to the active and say simply "the man beat the boy" = er-râgil ḍarab el-walad.

WORD LIST

Verbs			*Other words*	
fataḥ	(a)	= *open*	dât el-yôm	= *one day*
qafal	(u)	= *shut*	kursi	= *chair*
rasal	(i)	= *send*	qarîb	= *near*
heya		= *up*	sâyis	= *groom*
seket	(u)	= *be silent*	shâ'ir	= *poet*
			shubbak	= *window*

EXERCISE

(1) ya walad, ma teḍrabsh el-ḥimâr betâ'ek = **Boy, do not beat your donkey**
(2) ya bint, ma teskar es-saḥn da = **Girl, do not break this plate**
(3) ya bint, uskuti = **Girl, be silent**
(4) uqful el-bâb, ya walad = **Boy, shut the door**
(5) iftaḥ esh-shubbak, ya walad = **Boy, open the window**
(6) ente sâkin fên ? = **Where do you live ?**

(7) ana sâkin fi l'wasṭ el-medîne	= **I live in the middle of the city**
(8) hiye sâkine qarîb minnek	= **She lives near you**
(9) hum sâkinîn fi l'beled di	= **They live in this village**
(10) huwa gâlis 'andi	= **He is sitting at my side**
(11) hiya qâ'ide 'ala l'kursi	= **She is sitting on the chair**
(12) lâzimni 'êsh we-môya	= **I have need of bread and water**
(13) we-lâzimhum 'êsh keman	= **And they need bread also**
(14) huwa mâsik sigara fi îdu	= **He is holding a cigarette in his hand**
(15) ana ṭâlib mu'allim ṭayyib	= **I am looking for a good teacher**
(16) fih mu'allim ṭayyib qawi fi beledna, huwa esh-shêkh 'Abd el-Magîd, we-huwa 'âlim ketîr we-shâ'ir kemân	= **There is a very good teacher in our village, he is the sheikh Abd el-Magid, who is very learned and is a poet as well**
(17) khaddâmi qafalsh el-bâb ?	= **Has my servant shut the door ?**
(18) la, khaddâmek huwa keslân ketîr	= **No, your servant is very lazy**
(19) dât yôm we-huwa gâlis 'and abûna we-abûna huwa sâkit we-r-rigâl ketîr hum ḥaḍirîn	= **One day he was sitting by the side of our father and our father was silent and there were many men present**
(20) el-bâb maqfûl ?—la el-bab maftûḥ	= **Is the door shut ?—No, the door is open**
(21) ma teqfûlsh el-bâb, el-hawa ḥarr ketîr	= **Do not shut the door, the air is very hot**
(22) inzil min 'ala l-ḥiṣân	= **Dismount from the horse**

(23) ya walad, inzil min ʻala sh-shegare = **Boy, get down from the tree**

(24) ighsil idênek we-wishshek we-iqʻad ʻala l-kursi = **Wash your hands and face and sit down on the chair**

(25) ente, teqdirsh teʻrif kalâmi ?—Aiwa, ya sîdi, ana ʻârif kalâmek ḥaqq el-maʻarife = **Do you understand what I say ?—Yes, sir, I understand what you say very well**

(26) el-walad fên ?—huwa fi ôḍatna we-huwa qâʻid we-mâsik sigâra fi îdu = **Where is the boy ?—The boy is in our room sitting and holding a cigarette in his hand**

(27) huwa ʻâmil êy ?—mush aʻrif = **What is he doing ?—I do not know**

(28) ma tes'alnish = **Do not ask**

(29) esh huwa ʻâmal ? = **What is it he is doing ?**

(30) ḥaḍretek nâzil fi ey lokânda = **In what hotel is your honour staying**

(31) êsh huwa ṭâlib ? = **What is he looking for ?**

(32) nâzil maṭar ? = **Is it raining ?**

(33) el-maṭar nâzil shuwaiye = **It is raining just a little**

(34) el-mudîr qâʻid ʻala yêmîni = **The mudir is sitting on my right**

(35) inna li-llâh we-inna ilêh la-râgiʻîn = **To God we belong and to him verily we return**

(la- before verb or participle = " verily ".) (This sentence is conventional when it is perceived that anyone is near death.)

(36) lâ ḥôl we-lâ quwwa illa bi-llâh al-ʻali el-ʻaẓîm = **There is no might or power save in God the exalted and great**

(la " no " used here in the classical sense as " not ".) (Said in the presence of danger or before a very important undertaking.)

(37) sâmî‘ we-fâḥim = **(I am) hearing and understanding**

(= "to hear is to obey.")

(38) ea-sa‘a kam lâzin ashayya‘ ‘afshi ? = **At what hour must I send my luggage ?**

(39) heya ! heya ! ṭala‘et esh-shems = **Up, up, the sun has risen**

Chapter XV

THE THIRTEENTH LESSON—THE DERIVED STEMS OF THE VERB

So great is the regularity of word-building in Arabic that we are able to classify most forms containing more than three consonants (other than nouns borrowed from other languages) as having definite relations with the primary form of the three-consonant verb, and consequently much which in other languages would be catalogued in the dictionaries as separate words in Arabic may be reduced to a system and so the range of our vocabulary can be very easily extended. These derived forms of the verbs have the same tenses and persons as the ordinary three-consonant verbs, the only difference is that there is something added to the stem which affects the original meaning of the verb. After getting some idea of these derived verbal forms we shall find that the great majority of noun forms containing four or more consonants are themselves dependent on those derived verb stems, so that the subject enables us to make a very considerable extension of our vocabulary with very slight difficulty.

(1) The Stem with Doubled Medial (D)

Sometimes the basic three consonants are increased to four by doubling the middle one and this usually either intensifies the meaning or else makes a causative (i.e. the neuter verb becomes transitive), thus kasar = "break", kassar = "break into small pieces"; birik = "kneel", birrik =

"force anyone to kneel", etc. Very often, however, the four-consonant verb thus produced is in colloquial use but the original three-consonant form which occurs in classical Arabic is no longer current in the spoken language, and sometimes the four-consonant form is produced from a noun, as ṣabbin = "to use soap" from ṣabûn = "soap".

Properly the vowels in the Perfect of the stem with doubled medial are -a--a-, but if the final is not a "throat" letter the second vowel is often modified to -i-, at least in Egypt and Syria, and the first vowel is reduced to -e- (or -i-) under the usual conditions, thus barrik, ṣabbin, etc. The imperfect stem of these verbs of course needs two vowels and these are -a(e)--i-. The imperative uses this two-vowel stem of the imperfect and so does not require any prefixed or inserted vowel. The participle is mu-a--i- (e.g. mu'allim = "teacher", from 'allim = "teach", 'alim = "know"), the prefixed mu- often modified to me-, mi- in the colloquial. This may be illustrated by the following summary :—

	1st sing.	*2nd sing.*	*3rd sing.*
Perfect.	birrikt	birrikt	birrik
Imperfect.	abarrik	tebarrik	yebarrik
Imperative.	—	barrik	—
Participle.	mubarrik	—	—

(2) Shortened Form of the Doubled Medial (D*)

Sometimes the medial consonant is doubled and then one of the doubles falls away with compensating lengthening of the preceding vowel, thus birik becomes birrik (barrak) and then bârik, the distinctive feature being the first vowel long. In all other respects it follows the scheme already given for the doubled medial and if this is borne in mind there is nothing fresh to learn about this form. Thus :—

Perfect.	bârikt (bârakt) = *I blessed*
	bârik (bârak) = *He blessed*
Imperfect.	abârik, tebârik, yebarik, etc.
Imperative.	bârik, bâriku.
Participle.	mubârik.

(3) The Reflexive

The reflexive, which in modern colloquial often serves as the passive (cf. p. 118 above), is formed by prefixed t-, thus:—

(*a*) From the primary stem, as qafal = " lock ", itqafal = " be locked ", fataḥ = " open ", itfataḥ = " be opened ", etc. In the classical language this t- is transposed with the first consonant and so generally in 'Iraq and Syria, thus keteb = " write ", iktateb, etc. (It is important to notice that there is a dialectal difference in which iqtafal = itqafal, the meaning of both words being the same and the t- in both cases forming a reflexive from original qafal.) The scheme is:—

Perfect.	itqafal (iqtafal)
Imperfect (3rd sing.).	yitqifil (yiqtifil)
Imperative.	itqifil (iqtifil)
Participle.	mutqafil (muqtafil)

(*b*) The same reflexive t- can be added to the form with doubled medial (D above), thus tekallem = " converse ", from kallem = " speak ".

Perfect.	tekallem
Imperfect.	yetekellem (yetkellem)
Imperative.	tekellem (itkellem)
Participle.	muketellim

Thus taqarrab = " approach ", tenaddem = " regret ", etc. In Egyptian it is fairly common to find etnaddem for tenaddem, etkallem (or itkallem) for tekallem, etc.

(*c*) The reflexive t- may be added similarly to the reduced form of the doubled medial (D*) as tebarik, Egyptian itbarik, etc.

Perfect.	tebârik (itbârik)
Imperfect.	yetebârik (yetbârik)
Imperative.	tebârik (itbârik)
Participle.	mutebârik

So itshâgir = " quarrel " (Eg.).

(*d*) The reflexive may appear as ist-, the reflexive of the Causative which had s- in proto-Semitic (as we can see by survivals in various Semitic languages), but this s- after becoming h- finally weakened to '- and so produced forms such as 'ifqar or 'afqar = " make poor " from faqir = " be poor ", but verbs of this measure are so rare in the colloquial speech that it is hardly necessary to linger over them. In the reflexive the ancient s- has survived, and so we get :—

Perfect.	istaḥsen = " admire " (haṣun = " be beautiful ")
Imperfect.	yestaḥsin
Imperative.	istaḥsin
Participle.	mustaḥsin

This ist- form is rare as derivative from the regular three-consonant verb, but occurs more frequently with the verbs which have one of their consonants weak (w or y, see pp. 133, etc., below).

The formation of these derived stems has become rather a matter of lexicography than of grammar in the ordinary sense ; it is only because word-building in the Arabic follows such regular lines that we are able to include this subject within the limits of morphology at all. In the word lists we mark those forms which have doubled medials as (D), those which have had doubled medials but have reduced them with lengthening of the first stem vowel as (D*), and use (t) for the reflexive prefix, so that (Dt) describes such a form as tekellim or itkellim, (D*t) such as tebârik, or itbârik, and (st) such as istaḥsen.

All these derived forms are vocalised, as shown in the above summaries, with the ordinary modifications of -a- short to -e- and -i- according to dialect, and there is no difference due to derivation from primary qatal, qitil, or qutul.

Summary of this Lesson

Chief derived stems of verbs whose primary form is qatal, qitil, or qutul.

D. Type qattal (qettil). Intensive or transitive
D*. Type qâtal (qâtil). from intransitive primary.
t-. Reflexive (t) itqatel (iqtatal)
(Dt) taqattel (itqattel)
(D*t) taqâtel (itqâtel)
(st) istaqel

All these make their tenses and persons in the same way as the ordinary three-consonant verb.

EXERCISE

(Refer to vocabularies at end of book.)

(1) te'rif el-'arabi (el-loghet el-'arabiyye) ?—aiwa, a'rif shuwaiye	= **Do you know Arabic (the Arabic language)?—Yes, I know a little**
(2) fên te'allamt el-'arabi ?—fi Maṣr (el-Qâhire)	= **Where did you learn Arabic? —In Cairo**
(3) li tisa' ashhûr bass ate-'allim el-'arabi	= **I have been learning Arabic for nine months only**

(4) we-mîn ʻallimek ?—muʻallimi hûwa sh-shêkh ʻAbd el-Megîd	= And who has taught you ?—My teacher is the sheikh Abd el-Magid
(5) tetekellim bi-l-ʻarabi ?—ma aqdirsh atekellim ketîr	= Can you converse in Arabic ?—I cannot converse very much
(6) yumkin li taʻallum el-inkelîzi bi-ghêr muʻallim ?—yumkin, we-lâkin ʻala fikri da saʻab ketîr	= Could I learn English without a teacher ?—Perhaps, but I think it would be very difficult
(7) aḥsib el-loghet el-inkelîziyye mufîde giddan	= I consider that the English language is a very useful one
(8) ḥaḍḍiru l-khêl we-neḥammilha ana we-nte	= Bring here the horses and we will load them, you and I
(9) ahe el-khêl we-lâkin es-sâyis ma ḥaḍḍirshe ḥiṣânek	= Here are the horses, but the groom has not brought out your horse
(10) lêsh ma teḥaḍḍir el-khêl ḥalân ?	= Why did you not get the horses ready at once ?
(11) ana biddi asâfir ila d-dîr en-nehâr da	= I am going to travel to the monastery to-day
(12) ṭarîq es-selâme.—Allâh yesellimek	= (May it be) a journey of peace. — God give you peace
(13) mîn beyekhabbiṭ (bikhabbiṭ) ʻala l-bâb ?	= Who is knocking at the door ?
(14) ana mush musâfir wâḥadi	= I am not travelling alone
(15) sâfirt min Maṣr ila hêna we-maʼi ṣâḥibi we-sâyisna	= I have travelled from Cairo and with me is my friend and our groom
(16) tefaḍḍal (itfaḍḍel), el-ghadâ ḥâḍir	= Please enter, the dinner is ready

17) eḥna mabsûṭîn ketîr illi ente ma'na s-sâ'a di = **We are very pleased to have you with us at this time**

18) iḥteres ! = **Be careful !**

19) mîn teṭlub ?—ana ṭâlib el-khawâge (fulân) = **Who are you looking for ?—I am looking for Mr. N.**

20) el-bêt menaffaḍ = **The house is closed**

(The house is closed (=not at home). "maqful" not used in this connection as implying that the house is deserted, a very ill-omened suggestion.)

21) khâṭirek.—Allâh yesallim khâṭirek = **Your mind** (= farewell).—**God preserve your mind**

22) el-'abd ye'ammel we-r-rabbi yekemmel = **The slave** (=man) **plans, and the Lord carries out**

23) betefattish 'ala êy ? = **What are you disputing about ?**

24) kallimna bi-l-'arabi 'ala shân kalâmek yitfihim min kull ennâs = **Speak to us in Arabic so that what you say may be understood by everyone**

25) ana afahhimha lekun = **I will explain it to you**

26) ente bitḥammil ḥimârek ḥamla qadde keda teqîla leh ? = **Why are you loading your donkey with such a heavy burden ?**

27) khaddâmi ishtara bi-seb'a frank ghûk = **My servant bought cloth at seven francs**

28) 'Ali huwa kesser el-qulla = **It was Ali who broke the jug**

29) sharraftena = **You have honoured us**

(Salutation to guest, frequently repeated at any pause in the conversation.)

(*reply*) Allâh yeḥfaẓkum (-ek) = **May God protect you**

30) khâṭirek = **Your mind.** (=Good-bye)

(*reply*) Allâh yesallim khâṭirek = **God protect your mind**

31) ti'allamt el-'arabi fên ? = **Where did you learn Arabic ?**

32) tisallim li 'ala akhûk = **Remember me to your brother**

C.A.—5

(33) el-'abd yi'ammal we-r-Rabb yikemmel = **The slave** (=man) **plans and the Lord carries out**

(34) min beyekhabbet 'ala l-bâb ? = **Who is knocking at the door ?**

(35) betifattish 'ala êy ? = **What are you disputing about ?**

(36) ṭarîq es-salâme = **The journey of peace** (Farewell to a traveller)

(*reply*) Allâh yisellimek = **God give you peace**

(37) tesharraft bi-an aṣabbiḥ 'alêkum = **I have the honour to wish you good morning**

(38) Allâh yiṣabbiḥkum bi-l-khêr = **May God prosper the morning to you**

(39) ana mush musâfir waḥadi = **I am not travelling alone**

(40) sâfirt min Beirût ila l-Iskanderiya = **I travelled from Beirut to Alexandria**

(41) tefaḍḍal (itfaḍḍal) = **Please** (**sit down, eat, etc.**)

(42) itfaḍḍal ila l-baṭâṭa ô ghêrha min el-buqûl = **Please help yourself to potatoes or other vegetables**

(Or other than it of the vegetables.)

(43) itwakkil = **Commend yourself (to God)**

(Meaning, please go away.)

(44) el-bêt menaffeḍ = **The house is closed** (=not at home)

(Do not use "maqfûl", which is unpropitious in this connection.)

(45) astaghfir Allâh el-'aẓîm = **I ask pardon of God the great**

(Apology after breach of manners.)

(46) titkellem bi-l-'arabi ? = **Do you talk Arabic ?**

na'am ya khawâge atkallam shuwayye = **Yes, sir, I talk a little**

APPENDIX TO LESSON XIII

Table of derived stems including those rarely used in colloquial Arabic.

		Perf.	*Impf.*
I.	Primary (qatal, qitil, qutul)		
II.	(D) Intensive, etc.	qattal	yeqattil
III.	(D*) Intensive, etc.	qâtal	yeqâtil
IV.	Causative	'aqtal	yuqtil
			Rare in colloquial.
V.	Reflexive of II	taqattal (itqattal)	yeteqattal (yetqattal)
VI.	Reflexive of III	taqatal (itqatal)	yeteqatal (yetqatal)
VII.	Passive in n-	inqatal	yenqatil
			Rare in colloquial.
VIII.	Reflexive of I	iqtatal (itqatal)	yeqtatil
IX.	Colours, etc.	iqtall	yeqtall
			Rare.
X.	Reflexive of IV (st-)	istaqtal	yestaqil

Chapter XVI

THE FOURTEENTH LESSON—VERBS WITH WEAK INITIAL

As we have already seen, the Arabic verb normally is based on a root containing three consonants : but one of these may be a weak consonant such as w, y, or Hamza (', cf. p. 12) and that weak consonant may be merged in a neighbouring vowel, or else the second and third consonants may be alike. Any of these conditions may produce certain phonetic changes which have now to be considered, though those changes hardly deserve to be called " irregularities ".

First Radical Hamza

The first radical or root consonant may be Hamza, which is merely a check in the enunciation, and such a verb will appear as though commencing with a vowel, as amar = " command ", akal = " eat ", etc. In the ordinary way this has no effect in the perfect, but in the imperfect where the prefixed person is in contact with a vowel check the -a- of the prefix follows the general rule by which -a'- becomes -â-. It must be remembered that the te-, ye-, or ti-, yi-, etc., of the personal prefix was originally ta-, ya-, and so we get the personal prefixes of such verbs â-, tâ-, yâ-, nâ- as in âkul = " I eat ", tâkul = " thou eatest ", yâkul = " he eats ", nâkul = " we eat ", etc. In the active participle the Hamza becomes w- and so gives wâkil = " eating ", fem. wâkile, etc.

Perfect of (a)kal and (a)khad

The two verbs akal = " eat " and akhad = " take " commonly drop the first syllable in the perfect tense and reproduce the same process in the imperative. Thus :—

Perfect.	Sing.	1.		khadt	kalt
		2.	masc.	khadt	kalt
			fem.	khadti	kalti
		3.	masc.	khad	kal
			fem.	khadet	kalet
	Plur.	1.		khadna	kalna
		2.		khadtu	kalnu
		3.		khadu	kalu
Imperfect.	Sing.	1.		âkhud	âkul
		2.	masc.	tâkhud	tâkul
			fem.	tâkhudi	tâkuli
		3.	masc.	yâkhud	yâkul
			fem.	tâkhud	tâkul
	Plur.	1.		nâkhud	nâkul
		2.		tâkhudu	tâkulu
		3.		yâkhudu	yâkulu
Imperative.	Sing.		masc.	khud	kul
			fem.	khudi	kuli
	Plur.			khudu	kulu
Participle.	Act.			wâkhid	wâkil
	Pass.			—	mâkûl

From khad we get the derived (D*) akhiz (for akhidh) in the expression ma takhiznish = " do not blame me " used as introductory to a remark which might be resented as a liberty : from kal we have (D) wakkil = " cause to eat ", etc.

Verbs with Initial w-

In the perfect and participles verbs with initial w- are perfectly regular, thus waṣal = " arrive ", etc. In the imperfect the consonant -w- following the (original) -a- of the prefixed person naturally makes -o- which is the regular product of -aw- (see p. 13 above), but sometimes we may hear in the first person aw- (sounded like ow in "how"), and -u- (as a modification of -o-) in the other persons. Whether we get -o- or -u- is a matter of dialect and follows the general tendency of local speech. Taking as type waṣal = "arrive" we have :—

					or	
Imperfect	Sing.	1.		ôṣal	*or*	awṣal
		2.	masc.	tôṣal		tûṣal
			fem.	tôṣali		tûṣali
		3.	masc.	yôṣal		yûṣal
			fem.	tôṣal		tûṣal
	Plur.	1.		nôṣal		nûṣal
		2.		tôṣalu		tûṣalu
		3.		yôṣalu		yûṣalu

In the Imperative (which is always closely allied with the imperfect) the same phonetic principles are followed, thus :—

Imperative	sing.	masc.	ôṣal	ûṣal
		fem.	ôṣali	ûṣali
	plural		ôṣalu	ûṣalu

Verbs with First Radical y-

Verbs with first radical y- are rare. All that has been said above for verbs with initial w- holds good save that the prefixes in the imperfect of these verbs are ay-, tî-, yî-, nî- : thus yibis = "harden", imperfect aybas, tîbas, yîbas, nîbas, etc., and consistently with this the imperative îbas, îbasi, îbasu.

Derived Stems of Initial w/y Verbs

For the most part these derived forms are normal save that in the reflexive (t-) form we find ittaṣal for itwaṣal. Following this analogy khad gives reflexive ittâkhid, kal has ittâkil (D*t).

WORD LIST

kal (=akal)	= *eat*	'agal	= *speed*
khad (=akhad)	= *take*	'arabiya	= *cart, cab*
wagad	= *find, occur*	'askari	= *soldier*
waḥash	= *bereave*	ferkhe*	= *fowl*
waṣal	= *arrive*	'ilm	= *wisdom*
		samak	= *fish*
		sûq	= *market*

EXERCISE

(1) êsh tâkul ? = **What will you eat?**
(2) tâkul qalîl samak = **Eat a little fish**
(3) akhud qalîl, 'an iznak = **I will take a little, please**
(4) ente ma tâkulsh = **You are not eating**

(To guest pressing him to eat more.)

(5) ma aqdirsh âkul 'ala z-ziyâde = **I cannot eat any more**
(6) yûgad samak ketîr fi s-sûq ? = **Is there much fish in the market?**
(7) ma qadartish âgid samak fi s-sûq = **I could not find any fish in the market**
(8) nûṣil qabli ma yeghlaq es-sûq = **We came before the market closed**
(9) kul aktar = **Eat more**
(10) kul ka-ente fi bêtek = **Eat as if in your own house**
(11) min faḍlak, kul shuwayya min el-ferkhe di = **Please eat a little of this chicken**
(12) kewayyis ketîr = **It is excellent**
(13) waṣalni mektûbek = **I have received your letter**
(14) khadt felûs minnuh = **I took money from him**
(15) el-khabr esh-shûm yuṣal bi-l-'agal = **Bad news arrives with speed**

(16) huwa biyâkul êy ? = **What does he eat?**
(17) khud lek kisret khubz = **Take a morsel of bread**
(18) waḥashtena = **Thou hast made us lonely**

(To acquaintance after period of absence.)

(*reply*) allâh ma yûḥish fîk = **May God make no loneliness for thee**

(19) tefaḍḍal kul ma'na = **Please eat with us**
(20) ente ma kaltesh = **You have eaten nothing**
(21) ana shibi't = **I have had enough**
(22) kel kaza (Syr.=kul ka-da) = **Eat such as this**
(23) khudni ila l-khawâge (fulân) = **Take me to Mr. N.**
(24) khud 'ala yemînek = **Take (the way) to your right**
(25) yelzamek tâkhud 'arabîya = **You must take a cab**
(26) ya'ni ṭelibt el-khawâge ? = **Were you looking for the gentleman?**
(27) weṣelnâsh ? = **Have we arrived?**
(28) êsh kalt eṣ-ṣabâḥ da ? = **What have you eaten this morning?**
(29) ma kaltesh = **I have eaten nothing**
(30) bi-kâm âkhud el-kitâb da ? = **For how much shall I get this book?**
(31) ma yâkhudsh min ghêr felûs = **He takes nothing but money**
(32) kêf wagadtu ḥâl ṣâḥibkum ? = **How did you find your friend?**
(33) esh-shagar da ma yûgad illa fi dilâd el-maṣr = **This tree is not found in Egypt**
(34) mim mîn khadtûha ? = **Who did you get it from?**

(mim mîn = min mîn.)

(35) ma yosilni shayy minnuh = **I have received nothing from him**

(36) lahaqni el-'askari we-khadni	= **The soldier overtook me and took me away**
(37) kalabshuh we-khuduh	= **Handcuff him and take him away**
(38) kalû we-shirbû ḥadd shabi'û (Syr.)	= **They ate and drank until they had had enough**

(ḥadd = ḥatta.)

(39) khadt el-'ilm'anuh	= **I acquired knowledge of him**

CHAPTER XVII

THE FIFTEENTH LESSON—VERBS WITH WEAK MEDIAL

VERBS with weak medial are of two kinds (i) those with medial -w-, as q-w-l, and (ii) those with medial -y-, as g-y-b. We need not consider those with medial Hamza as either the Hamza remains and so the verb is regular, or else it becomes w/y and so it falls within one of the classes given above.

VERBS WITH MEDIAL W: PERFECT

Verbs with medial -w- merge that medial in the neighbouring vowel sounds and so form one syllable. Before one consonant -awa- becomes -â-, and before two consonants -u-: thus qâl (for qawal), qâlet (for qawalet), qâlu (for qawalu); and qult (for qawalt), qulti (for qawalti), qulna (for qawalna), and qultu (for qawaltu). Such verbs appear in the vocabulary as words of one syllable, e.g. qâl = "he said", and after them is noted the root form (qwl, etc.). The formation of the persons is regular in all respects. Thus:—

qult = *I said*
qult = *thou saidest*
qulti = *thou* (fem.) *saidest*
qâl = *he said*
qâlet = *she said*
qulna = *we said*
qultu = *you said*
qâlu = *they said.*

In Lower Egypt, Syria, etc., the above becomes 'ult, 'ulti, etc., as stated on pages 18–19 (c) above: so in the following a'ul, te'ul, etc.

Imperfect.

In the imperfect these verbs have vowel -u-, and this with the -w- makes -û-, so we have :—

aqûl = *I speak*
teqûl = *thou speakest*
teqûli = *thou* (fem.) *speakest*
yeqûl = *he speaks*
teqûl = *she speaks*
neqûl = *we speak*
teqûlu = *you speak*
yeqûlu = *they speak*

In 'Iraq the plural termination -u may, as usual, be heard with final -n.

Imperative.

In the imperative no prefixed vowel is needed as the one initial consonant is vocalized by the stem vowel, so we have :—

Sing.	*masc.* qûl	*fem.* qûli
Plural	qûlu	

Participle.

The active participle is qâyil (for classical qâ'il): the passive participle is not in use.

Derived Stems.

The (D) stem, qawwal, etc., is perfectly regular, in the (t) and (st) we find long -a- shortening before two consonants, thus (t) itqâl, itqalt, etc., *impf.* yetqâl, (st) istaqâl, istaqalt, etc., *impf.* yestaqîl.

These verbs with medial w form a very important group, most are as qâl above, but a few, e.g. nâm = "sleep", make imperfect with -â- instead of -û-, thus anâm, tenâm, etc. The verb kân, kunt, etc., *impf.* yekûn, is in general use to denote the verb " to be " when in the past or future time, in the present of course no such verb is needed, thus ana kunt keslân = " I was lazy ", huwa kân ta'bân = " he was tired ", etc. Kân râgil fi medîna min el-medayn eṣ-ṣîn = " there was a man in a certain city in China ", ente tekûn 'aṭshân = " you will be thirsty ", etc. This verb added to the tenses of other verbs produces a new tense system which figures in modern Arabic. The free use of kan as the verb " to be " seems to be a development—at least we assume so from the total absence of this verb, at least in that sense, in the other Semitic languages—but it is introduced freely in the colloquial, often, it must be confessed, where the sentence would be just as good without it. Its use in forming a tense system will be dealt with later (see Lesson XX), to a large extent that seems to be a development due to those who have come under the influence of European education and is somewhat artificial and " bookish " ; it is doubtful if we ought to go further than to say that in the vernacular the perfect of kân is used for past time, the imperfect for the future, leaving schemes of pluperfect, future perfect, etc., for those who are trying to twist the Semitic character of Arabic to fit into the totally different structure of the Indo-European languages. ṣâr also is used in the sense " to be " : dâm is " to be " in the sense of " continue ", as ma dumt = " as long as I am . . ." The verb qâm = " rise " is also used as a kind of auxiliary meaning " begin ", thus qâm qâl = " he began to say ", etc. —the frequent use of qâm and kân is characteristic of the narrative in the speech of the people, folk tales, and the stories in the " Thousand Nights and a Night " begin almost every sentence with qâm or kân, often quite superfluous. 'âz occurs most often in the participle 'âwiz (= 'ôz) = " want, need ", thus ente 'âwiz êy ? = " what do you want ? " ana 'âwiz sikkîn = " I want a knife ", etc. The verb râd in the derived form arâd (causative, No. IV on p. 131) is a useful verb meaning " desire, want " used before another verb, thus turîd aqaddam lek 'êsh ? = " would you like me to give you some bread ? ", turîd teqûl êh ? = " what do you want to say ? ", etc. We have already noted the use of the participle râyiḥ = " going " (from râḥ) as giving a future sense to the sentence in which it is used. (Cf. p. 109 above.)

EXAMPLES

êsh huwa 'âwiz ?—ma anîsh 'ârif êsh huwa 'âwiz	= *What does he want ?—I do not know what he wants.*
fâtetni el-furṣe	= *The opportunity escaped me.*
el-qôm kulluhum mâtu min el-gû'	= *All the people died of hunger.*
el-mu'allim lâm fikri	= *The teacher disapproved my opinion.*
li sene kâmile ma shuftush	= *I have not seen him for a whole year (= to me a complete year I have not seen him).*
êsh bitqûl ente ?	= *What do you say ?*

Verbs with Medial y : Perfect

The verbs with medial -y- follow the lines already indicated for those with medial -w- : where those verbs made -â- so do these, where they made -u- these make -i-, and where they made -û- these make -î-. The example we take is the verb gâb = " bring ". Classical Arabic had a verb gâ' = " go ", to which we shall refer later (cf. p. 150), followed by the preposition bi- this had the sense of "bring" and thence modern Arabic has formed the verb gâb in all respects as though g-y-b.

gibt = *I brought*
gibt = *thou broughtest*
gibti = *thou* (fem.) *broughtest*
gâb = *he brought*
gâbet = *she brought*
gibna = *we brought*
gibtu = *you brought*
gâbu = *they brought*

Imperfect.

The imperfect has stem vowel -i- (= -yi-), thus:—

agîb = *I bring*
tegîb = *thou bringest*
tegîbi = *thou* (fem.) *bringest*
yegîb = *he brings*
tegîb = *she brings*
negîb = *we bring*
tegîbu = *you bring*
yegîbu = *they bring*

Imperative.

Sing. gîb *fem.* gîbi
Plur. gîbu

Participle.

gâyib (gêyib), etc.

Derived Stems.

The stem with doubled medial (D) and (D*) offers nothing abnormal, gayyib, gayib, etc., the -y- here appearing as a consonant: in the reflexive (t) and (st) we get the same resultants as in the medial -w- verbs, thus (t) itgab, itgabt, *impf.* yugib, (st) istagab, istagabt, *impf.* yestabib, etc.

These medial -y- verbs are not so numerous or so useful as those with medial -w-, indeed gab is the only one which frequently enters into ordinary speech.

WORD LIST

Verbs

'âd	(w)	= *take refuge*
'âsh	(w)	= *live*
'âz	(w)	= *need*
dâḥ	(w)	= *be dizzy*
dâkh	(w)	= *humble*
fahim	(st-)	= *inquire*
faragh		= *be emptied*
feṣah		= *stride*
tefessaḥ		= *stroll*
fât	(w)	= *pass by*
gâb	(y)	= *bring, give*
kâl	(y)	= *measure*
kân	(w)	= *be*
khâf	(w)	= *fear*
kenes		= *sweep*
qâl	(w)	= *say*
qâm	(w)	= *arise, begin*
râḥ	(w)	= *go*
rekab		= *mount, ride, embark*
ṣâm	(w)	= *fast*
ṣâr	(w)	= *be*
shâ'		= *will*
shâf	(w)	= *see*
ṭâl	(w)	= *be long,* (D) *lengthen*
zâd	(w)	= *increase*

Other Words

'afrîṭ	= *demon*
amsak	= *constipation*
bâbûr	= *steamer*
ba'd	= *after*
bustân	= *garden (pers.)*
dîr	= *monastery (Christian)*
dughri	= *straight on*
dohr	= *noon*
embariḥ	= *yesterday*
fe-	= *and, and so*
falaq	= *dawn*
fellaḥ (-în)	= *cultivator of the soil*
gubba*	= (*name of a garment*)
ḥalân	= *at once*
honak	= *there*
ḥarîr	= *silk*
ḥatta	= *until, up to*
ibriq	= *jug*
in	= *if*
lamma	= *when*
lisân	= *tongue*
makhzen*	= *store*
meqlûb	= *savage*
marra*	= *woman*
mesrûr	= *pleased*
qufl	= *lock*
qaribân	= *nearly*
ragîm	= *stoned (of the devil)*
rîḥ	= *wind*
ṣabun	= *soap*
safir	= *traveller*
sudr	= *chest*
sene (sinin)	= *year*
shahr	= *month*
sharbe*	= *drink*
sharr	= *harm*
tasht	= *basin*

EXERCISE

(1) qâl ṣâḥib ed-dâr min bel-bâb ? =	**The master of the house said, Who is at the door?**

(bel-=bi-l-.)

(2) sa'alni we-qâl li, min ên ente ?—w-êsh qult ente ? =	**He asked me saying, Where do you come from?—And what did you say?**
(3) we-qâl el-ḥammâl, Da nehâr mubârak we-nehâr sa'id =	**And the porter said, This is a blessed and happy day**
(4) wi-'al li, lêh ?	**And he said to me, Why?**

(Dialect of Lower Egypt, 'al=qal.)

(5) wâḥid fellaḥ fi Dêrût qâl li, Ana shufti marra wâhid min el-'afârit =	**A certain fellah in Deirut said to me, Once I saw one of the afarit**
(6) ma tequlish kida =	**Do not talk like that**
(7) emta esh-shêkh ṣâḥibek kharag ?—kân el-waqt qariban ed-dohr =	**When did the sheikh who is your friend go out?—The time was about noon**
(8) qâm qâl er-râgil li-s-sâfir, Ente râyiḥ fên ? =	**The man began saying to the traveller, Where are you going?**
(9) esh-shêkh huwa marîḍ 'ala khâṭir we 'ala fikri râyiḥ yemût =	**The sheikh is seriously ill and I think he is going to die**
(10) er-râgil qâm ḥalân we-rigi' ila ṣâḥibuh =	**The man stood up at once and went back to his friend**
(11) rakebt bâbûr el-Brindîzi illi yeqûlû 'alêh =	**I embarked on the Brindisi steamer they talk about**
(12) huwa yerûḥ ila ên ?—yerûḥ ila 'azvetuh—ente rûḥ waiyyâh =	**Where is he going?—He is going to his farm. Do you go with him**

(13) kân lâbis gubba ḥarîr = **He was wearing a silk jubbeh**

(14) a'ûz akallimek—yekul ḥaḍretek, ana sâmi = **I want to have a word with you. Let your honour speak, I am listening**

(15) ente dawwakht râsi = **Thou hast humbled my head**

(16) da, êsh ismuh ?—qul min tâni—mush taman = **What is the name of this ?—say it again—that's not quite right**

(17) ente 'âwiz êsh ?—ana 'âwiz sharbe 'alishân 'andi amsak = **What do you want ?—I want a draught because I have constipation**

(18) kunt ente fên embariḥ ?—ana kunt (kutt) fi s-sûq-we-akhûk fên ?—huwa kân fi l-gâmi' ma' abûna = **Where were you yesterday ?—I was in the market.—And your brother, where was he ?—He was in the mosque with our father**

(19) qâm ila el-makhzen we-fataḥuh fe-kilna ḥatta faragh el-makhzen = **He went to the magazine and opened it and we measured it (= its contents) until it was empty**

(20) qum, ya ṣâḥibi, nergi' ila dârna = **Rise, my friend, let us go back to our house**

(21) mîn minkum yekûn luh ṣâḥib = **Who of you has a friend ?**

(22) rûḥu bina netefessaḥ, en-nehâr da shemm en-nesîm = **Go with us for a stroll, to-day is the Shem en-Nesim**

(23) râsi dâyiḥ we-ma aqdirsh akteb = **My head is dizzy and I cannot write**

(24) qul, we-lâkin ma teṭawwilshe lisânek = **Speak, but do not prolong thy speech**

(25) ruḥna l-beled ('ashan) nistafhim	= **We went to the town to make inquiry**

(The use of ashan (ala shan) is optional.)

(26) ente fâhim ana baqûl êy ?	= **Do you understand what I say?**
(27) ya 'awwaḍ Allâh	= **May God compensate**

(Street cry of the water seller.)

(28) ruḥ dughri	= **Go straight on**
(29) ya nâs, khâfu min Allâh	= **O men, fear God**
(30) kân râgil ṣayyâd we-kân kebîr fi s-sinîn we-luh zôge we-talât awlad we-huwa faqîr el-ḥâl	= **There was a man who was a fisherman and he was advanced in years and had a wife and three sons and he was poor in circumstances**
(31) in kân honâk huwa aq'ad ma'uh we-in ma kanshe argi' ila hena	= **If he is there I will stay with him and if he is not I will come back here**
(32) lamma kutt (kunt) ṣughayyir	= **When I was a little boy**
(33) ya walad, kunt keslân qawi	= **Boy, you have been very idle**
(34) kan maṭar fi l-lêle we-kânet er-rîyâḥ shedîde qawi	= **There was rain in the night and the wind was very rough**
(35) arba'a we-talâta gâbu kâm ?	= **How much do four and three make?**
(36) ma dumt ḥaiy	= **As long as I live**
(37) kullima huwa ṭaiyib ṣâr ghâli	= **Everything that is good is dear**
(38) fâtet et-telâte	= **It is past three o'clock**
(39) ṣâmu ila l-gherûb	= **They fasted until sunset**
(40) Allâh yezîd faḍlek	= **God increase your welfare**

(41) ‘âwiz minni êy, ya walad ? = **What do you want of me, boy?**

(42) huwa khâf ketîr = **He was very much afraid**

(43) ana mesrûr li-anni shuftek = **I am pleased to have seen you**

(44) in ‘isht argi‘ bi-t-tâni = **If I live I will go back again**

(45) Maḥmûd, gîb eṭ-ṭasht we-l-ibrîq môya we-ṣ-ṣâbûn li-nighsil yedêna (îdêna) = **Mahmud, bring the basin and a jug of water and the soap for us to wash our hands**

(46) a‘ûd billâh min esh-shaiṭân er-ragîm = **I seek refuge with God from the stoned devil**

(Apology made after yawning ; the back of the left hand is placed before the mouth during a yawn. The reference is to the stoning of the pillars which represent the devil (?), a rite performed during the latter part of the greater pilgrimage.)

(47) a‘ûd bi-rabb el-falaq = **I take refuge with the Lord of the dawn**

(Apology after improperly expressing admiration of a child or of any article in one's host's possession. The words are the opening phrase of the 113th Sura and the words next following (which need not be said) are regarded as an exorcism of evil spirits.)

(48) ma shayy sharr in shâ’ allâh = **It is no harm, if God wills**

(Form of condolence on visiting a sick person.)

(49) ma shâ‘ allâh = **It is what God pleases**

(Expression of admiration on seeing anything pleasant.)

(50) yekun lek ‘ashrîn riyâl fi sh-shahr = **You shall have twenty dollars a month**

(51) tekunshe hêna ba‘de bukra es-sâ‘a telâte ?—na‘am, akun hêna es-sâ‘a da = **Will you be here at three o'clock the day after to-morrow ?—Yes, I shall be here at that time**

(52) ma terûḥsh ma‘ er-râgil da = **Do not go with that man**

(53) râḥ yeshûf abûh = **He went to see his father**

(54) ma baqûlsh ḥâge (Eg.) = **I say nothing**

(55) kull en-nâs biqûlû kida = **Everyone says so**

(56) qâm gâwabuh = **He began answering him**

(57) aye elli bete'ûzuh ? = **What is it you want ?**

(58) kenes bêti we-râḥ li-l-bustân = **He swept my room and went into the garden**

(59) el-khaddâm khâf el-kelb el-meqlûb = **The servant was afraid of the savage dog**

(60) êsh kân fi qufl el-bâb ? = **What was in the lock of the door ?**

(61) râḥ marîḍ min sudruh = **He has been taken ill in his chest**

(62) kân fi medîne min medâyin aṣ-Ṣîn râgil khayyâṭ faqîr we-kân luh walad ismuh 'Ala' ed-Dîn fe-hada l-walad kân ma'kus min ṣigharuh = **There was in a certain city of China a man who was a tailor and poor, and he had a son called 'Ala' ad-Din, and this boy was unfortunate from his childhood**

(63) ma 'am beghder (= ma qam baqdar, dial. of Damascus) = **I cannot**

(64) ba'ref beddak t'qûl = **I know you will say**

(65) hiye betnâm bi-franga 'ala t-takheṭ, ana b'nâm bel-mrabba' 'al arḍ = **She sleeps in a bed on the first floor, I sleep in the basement on the ground**

(These three passages, 63–5, are from M. le commandant Malinjoud's *Textes en dialecte de Damas* (Journal Asiat. cciv, p. 295, etc.). They are taken from a consultation in which an uneducated woman of Damascus appeals to a doctor and represent the dialect of the illiterate. Note q=' in one place and in another =gh, also observe the way in which the vowels are "swallowed".)

Chapter XVIII

THE SIXTEENTH LESSON—VERBS WITH FINAL WEAK

Verbs with Final Weak (Class III)

Some verbs have final -y or -w or -' (assimilating to -y) and normally this with -a- becomes -e (= ay) before a consonant or -â final; with -i- it becomes -i, with -u- it becomes -u. Thus:—

qarayt	becomes	qarêt
qaray	,,	qarâ
qarayu	,,	qarû
aqriy	,,	aqrî, etc.

These phonetic changes may be illustrated by qaray (for classical qara' "read") and mashiy = "walk".

Perfect.

		masc.	*fem.*	*masc.*	*fem.*
Sing.	1.	qarêt		mishît	
	2.	qarêt	qarêti	mishît	mishîti
	3.	qarâ	qarit	mishî	mishyit
Plur.	1.	qarêna		mishîna	
	2.	qarêtu		mishîtu	
	3.	qarû		mishîyu	

(The only exceptional peculiarities to be noted are the 3rd fem. sing. and the 3rd plur. of the -i- verbs.)

Imperfect.

Sing.	1.	aqrî		amshî	
	2.	tiqrî	tiqrî	timshî	timshî
	3.	yiqrî	tiqrî, etc.	yimshî	timshî, etc.

Imperative.

Sing.	iqrî	imshî
Plur.	iqrû	imshû

(In 'Iraq the -a- is retained in the Imperfect aqrâ, taqra, etc., but the -i- verbs are as above.)

Special Note on the Verb ga "come"

The verb gâ was originally gaya and so had weak medial and final. We have already met this verb in its modern derivative gab. Gâ is thus conjugated :—

Perfect.

		masc.	*fem.*	
Sing.	1.	gêt (gît)		*I came*
	2.	gêt (gît)	gêti (gîti)	*thou camest*
	3.	gâ (gîh)	gat	*he, she came*
Plur.	1.	gêna (gîna)		*we came*
	2.	gêtu (gîtu)		*you came*
	3.	gû		*they came*

Imperfect.

Sing.	1.	âgî		*I come*
	2.	tîgî	tîgî	*thou comest*
	3.	yîgî	tîgî	*he, she comes*
Plur.	1.	nîgî		*we come*
	2.	tîgû		*you come*
	3.	yîgû		*they come*

Participle.

Act. gây, (gê), *fem.* gâye, *plur.* gâyîn.

The imperative of this verb is not in use: instead we employ :—

Sing.	*masc.*	ta'âla (tâ'a)
	fem.	ta'âli (tâ'i)
Plur.		ta'âlu (tâ'a)

Notes

We have already (p. 109 above) noted that mâshî (= mashiy), the active participle of the verb mishî, is used as an auxiliary to produce a future sense. The verb baqâ = " remain " is also often used in conjunction with other verbs and conveys the meaning of " become, begin to ", etc., thus baqa yiḍrab fîh = " he began to beat him ", baqa yishrab = " he went on drinking ", baqet mablûl = " I became wet ", etc. So gâ can often imply " become, be ", as in lamma gêt arûḥ = " when I came to go ", i.e. " just as I was about to go ". The verb shâ is really one with medial weak (shâ'), but the final Hamza tending to become -y it rather appears as one with both medial and final weak making shâ, *imperfect* ashâ, teshâ, etc. (with -â in the imperf.-imperative) : it occurs most commonly in the expression in shâ allâh = " if God wills ".

WORD LIST

Verbs

‘aṭâ	= *give*	khallâ	= *compel*
baqâ	= *preserve* *continue*	laqâ	= *meet*
		mishî	= *run, go*
daḥak	= *laugh*	nesâ	= *forget*
fadâ	= *be free*	qarâ	= *read*
gâ	= *come*	saḥim	= *preserve*
garâ	= *run away*	ṣallâ	= *pray*
hadâ (yahdi)	= *guide*	sharâ	= *buy* (*see* ishtara)
hanî	= *profit*	ta‘âla, ta‘a	= *come* (*imperative*)
iddâ	= *give*		
ishtarâ	= *buy*	wafî	= *depart, die*
khabbir	= *tell*	tûffâ	= *cause to die*

Other Words

adi	= *behold*	mudabbir	= *ruler*
budd	= *assuredly*	mekân	= *place*
‘êniyye	= *sample*	muntaṣaf	= *middle*
ghêt	= *field*	ra‘i	= *grazing*
ḥinma	= *whenever*	sîf	= *sword*
ḥayna	= *short while*	ta‘âla	= *high* (*of God*)
kerîm	= *generous*	tâbi‘	= *follower*
khalq	= *creation*	ṭalû‘	= *rising* (*of sun*)
kharûf	= *lamb*	ẓalâm	= *darkness*
leben	= *milk*		

EXERCISE

(1) agât li gawâb ?	= **Is there a letter for me?**
(2) tûfî wâlidhum we-khalaf luhum mâl ketîr	= **Their father died and left them much wealth**
(3) we-lamma tûffâh Allâh ta'âlâ	= **And when God Most High took him**
(4) ana baqêt min etbâ 'uh	= **I am one of his followers**
(5) mesît ismuh	= **I have forgotten his name**
(6) mishi shuwayia we-qâm rigi'	= **He went a little way and began to turn back**
(7) lamma mishi zeyyi mîl	= **When he had gone about a mile**
(8) emta gêt ?	= **When did you come?**
(9) we-kêf gêt ?—gêt mâshi	= **And how did you come?—I came on foot**
(10) hûwa yigî en-nehârde ?	= **Does he come to-day?**
(11) mîn qâl lek tigî ?	= **Who told you to come?**
(12) ma tigîsh en-nehârde	= **Do not come to-day**
(13) ta'âla hêna	= **Come here**
(14) la budd ma yegi	= **He is sure to come**
(15) ḥadesh gâ ?	= **Has anyone come?**
(16) gâ ila Deirût fi muntaṣaf as-sâ'a t-tâlta	= **He came to Deirut about three o'clock**
(17) huwa mashi fi-s-sikka	= **He is walking along the road**
(18) tûfi wâlidi fe-ṣirt simsâr mekânuh	= **My father died and I became a broker in his place**
(19) akhrag mandîl we-fîh qadr semsem we-qâl Kâm yesâwi el-ardebb min da ?	= **He took out a handkerchief in which was a measure of sesame and said, How much is that worth by the ardebb?**
(20) fe-qult luh, Mâye dirhem	= **And I said to him, A hundred dirhems**

(21) fe-qâl li, Khud et-terrâṣîn we-l-keyyâlîn we-i'mid ila bâb en-Nasr ila khân el-Gawali = **And he said to me, Get the carriers and measurers and go towards the Victory Gate to the Gawali Khan**

(22) a'ṭâni es-semsem bi-mandîluh illi fîh el-'êniyye = **In his handkerchief he gave me the sesame which was the sample**

(23) fe-gâ kull ardebb bi-mâyet we-'ashrîn dirhem = **And each ardebb came to a hundred and twenty dirhems**

(24) gâ l-kharûf ye'allim abûh el-ra'i = **The lamb came to teach his father how to graze**

(Proverbial expression. el-ra'i = " grazing ", verbal noun.)

(25) iddîni l-list = **Give me the menu**

(26) yinî êy ? = **What does it mean ?**

(27) rabbuna kerîm, we-hûwa el-mudabbir hal yumkin yansî khalquh ? = **Our Lord is generous, he is the ruler—will he perchance forget his creatures ?**

(28) el-ḥamdu lillâh = **Praise be to God**

(*reply*) saḥimkum allâh = **God save you**

(*ans.*) yehdâna we-yehdâkum allâh = **God guide us and you**

(This is said when anyone sneezes. Those who hear him make the reply, and he who sneezed gives the answer.)

(29) abqâkum allâh = **God preserve you**

(*reply*) allâh yebqîkum = **And may he preserve you**

(30) rûḥ ishtari shuwaiya qahwa = **Go and buy some coffee**

(31) li-yahnîk = **May it profit you**

(*reply*) yehannîk allâh = **May God make it wholesome for you**

(Said on offering coffee to a guest, and guest's reply.)

(32) ta'âla ma'i ila el-medîna = **Come with me to the city**

(33) hallâni amshi ma'uh = **He made me walk with him**
(34) ente fâdi en-nehâr da ? = **Are you free to-day?**
(35) Allâh ye'ṭîk = **God give to thee**

(Form of refusal to a beggar.)

(36) warrînî . . . = **Show me . . .**
(37) warrînî kharâṭa li-sh Shâm = **Show me a map of Syria**
(38) ta'a ya gada' (vulg.) = **Come here, my fine fellow**
(39) ṣallî 'an-nabi (='ala n-nabi) = **Bless the Prophet**

(After anyone has improperly expressed admiration for anything.)

(*reply*) allâhum ṣalli 'alêh = **God bless him**

(Strictly ṣalla=" prayer ", here no doubt " blessing ".)

(40) ma sha' allâh = **(It is) what God wills**

(The more proper way of expressing admiration of anything seen.)

(41) ṣallu (ṣalli) 'an-nabi = **Bless the Prophet**

(Invitation by bystander to check those who are in angry dispute.)

or eṣ-ṣala 'an-nabi = **Blessing on the Prophet**

(Reply as above.)

(42) ba'd ma bîṣalli = **After he had said his prayers**
(43) baqêt ḥayna fi Maṣr = **I stayed a short time in Egypt**
(44) er-rasûl allâh ṣallât Allâh 'alêh we-salâm = **The Apostle of God, may the the blessing of God be on him and peace**

(This is the proper way of making reference to Muhammad. If the speaker does not add the invocation some bystander usually repeats it in a low voice.)

(45) yeminek tigi = **You can come**
(46) ente gây min êy ? = **Where are you coming from?**
(47) adîni gît = **Behold, I have come**
(48) gâ fi ṣ-ṣabâḥ = **He came in the morning**
(49) gâ we-b-îduh sîf = **He came with a sword in his hand**

(50) gêt ma‘ ṭalû‘ esh-shems = **I came at sunrise**

(51) kân yimshi fi s-sikka fi zalâm el-lêl fe-khâf shuwayya = **He was going along the road in the darkness of the night and he was rather frightened**

(52) kutt amshi li-l-ghêt betâ‘i we-lamma ashûf el-ḥarâmi fegirêt minnuh = **I was going to my field and when I saw the thief I ran away from him**

(53) ta‘rif teqrâ ?—na‘am, ya khawâge (khôge) = **Are you able to read?—Yes, sir**

(54) fi êy kitâb ente teqrâ dilwaqt (el-ân) ? = **What book are you reading now?**

(55) Ana aqrâ el-ân fi kitâb " esh-Shawqiyât " = **I am reading now the Shawkiyat**

(56) ṭayyib, Shawqi Bey huwa shâ‘ir ṭayyib qawi, we lâkin ‘ala fikri el-kitâb da ṣa‘ab ‘alêk = **Good, Shawki Bey is an excellent poet, but in my opinion that book is too difficult for you**

(57) ḥinma ana ûṣal ila Miṣr arsil lek kitâb kuwayyis = **When I go to Cairo I will send you a good book**

(58) kânet betidḥak ‘ala êy ? = **What was she laughing at?**

(59) sherît laḥm baqar we-leben fi s-sûq = **I bought beef and milk in the market**

(60) warrîni kêfâsh nekhar-reghum min hêna = **Show me how we can get them out of here**

(61) iza telâqît ma‘ ‘Ali khabbiruh yegîni = **If you meet Ali tell him to come to me**

(62) qul luh yegi ḥâlan = **Tell him to come soon**

(63) râḥ yegi bukra = **He will come to-morrow**

(64) eddîni shuwaiya ziyâde = **Give me a little of the same**

(65) we-fi tâni yôm gâ kemân = **And the next day he came again**

(66) ta‘al bass = **Come, that will do**

Chapter XIX

THE SEVENTEENTH LESSON—VERBS WITH REPEATED MEDIAL: MODERN TENSE FORMS

Verbs of Type ḥarr "be hot"

Verbs in which the second and third consonants of the root are the same show certain contractions. Thus:—

			Perfect.	*Imperfect.*	*Imperative.*
Sing.	1.		ḥarrêt	aḥirr	
	2.	*masc.*	ḥarrêt	teḥirr	ḥirr
		fem.	ḥarrêti	teḥirri	ḥirri
	3.	*masc.*	ḥarr	yeḥirr	
		fem.	ḥarrit	teḥirr	
Plur.	1.		ḥarrêna	neḥirr	
	2.		ḥarrêtu	teḥirru	ḥirru
	3.		ḥarru	yeḥirru	

It will be perceived that verbs of this kind imitate those with final weak and so make a kind of compensation for the loss of a vowel between the doubled consonants.

MG.

ʻadd (i)	= *count*
gall	= *avert*
ḥabb (i)	= *like, love*
ḥagg	= *go on pity*
ḥall	= *descend*
ḥarr	= *be hot*
khaṣṣ	= *concern*
lamm	= *pick up*
madd	= *stretch out*
ṣaḥḥ	= *awake*
shaqq	= *visit (medical, etc.)*

ẓann (n)	= *suppose*
baṭu	= *stomach*
fumm	= *mouth* (lit.)
ḥanaq	= ,, (mod.)
ghaṭâ	= *cover*
girdôn	= *field mouse*
gabîḥ	= *untrustworthy*
ṣâdiq	= *honourable, upright*
ṣâni' (ṣunnâ')	= *craftsman*

EXERCISE

(1) ḥallet el-barke bi-qudûmek	= **Blessing descended at your approach**
(2) (*reply*) allâh yubârak fîk	= **May God bless you**
(3) ida (iza) kân yeḥibb	= **If he likes**
(4) teḥibb shuwaiyya min el-farâkh da ?	= **Would you like a little of this fowl ?**
(5) yegallek allâh	= **May God avert (it) (from) you** (after mentioning any disaster, etc.)
(6) êsh teḥibb takul ?	= **What would you like to eat ?**
(7) fi muṣṣ min el-lêl ṣaḥḥ el-walad min nûm we-qâl Ana 'eṭshân, we-kân ibrîq el-môya 'anduh we-shirib min el-môya, we-lâkin el-ibrîq dâk huwa min ghêr ghaṭâ we-nizil fi fummuh girdôn saghîr we-lamma el-walad shirib min el-ibrîq dâk nizil el-girdôn da fi baṭnuh	= **In the middle of the night the boy awoke from sleep and said, I am thirsty, and there was a jug of water by him and he drank of the water. But that jug was without a cover, and a little field mouse had gone down into its mouth and when the boy drank from that jug this field mouse went down into his stomach**

(8) ḥasib, ma tebukhkhinish bi-l-moya	= **Look out—do not splash me with the water**
(9) teḥibb el-khubz (-esh) ?	= **Would you like some bread ?**
(10) el-muslimin yeḥiggu fi shahr el-Ḥigga	= **Muslims make the pilgrimage in the month of el-Higga**
(11) midd îdek we-limmiha min 'ala l-arḍ	= **Put out your hand and take it up from the ground**
(12) ẓannêtuh râgil ṣâdiq	= **I supposed him an upright man**
(13) ma kuntish aẓunnek râgil qabîḥ kide	= **I did not think you were such an untrustworthy man**
(14) huwa ẓannek ṣâni' mâhir	= **He thought you a skilful craftsman**
(15) ẓannêtna ṣunnâ' mâhirîn ?	= **Did you suppose us to be skilled craftsmen ?**
(16) da ma yekheṣṣenâsh	= **That does not concern us**
(17) ṣert tisheqq 'alîye ('alîye = 'alêya)	= **You used to visit me**

The Verb—Supplementary, Modern Tense Forms

We now turn to the tense formations which have been developed in modern Arabic, some of them more or less the fictions of the educated who have been trying (mistakenly) to press Arabic into the tense scheme which has been evolved in the Indo-European languages and which is really not adapted to Arabic. Still, however, it has a certain vogue and can be employed in the expression of time, so should not be altogether ignored.

(i) *Pluperfect.*

The pluperfect "I had written", etc., can be expressed by using the perfect of kan with the perfect of another verb, thus :—

kunt ketebt = *I had written*
kân keteb = *he had written*
kânet ketebet = *she had written*
kunna ketebna = *we had written*, etc.

(ii) *The Imperfect.*

The European imperfect "I was writing", etc., can be expressed—

(*a*) By using the perfect of kan with the imperfect of another verb—

kunt akteb = *I was writing*
kân yekteb = *he was writing*, etc.

(*b*) By using the perfect of kan with the active participle—

kunt kâtib = *I was writing*
kân kâtib = *he was writing*
kânet kâtibe = *she was writing*
kunna kâtibîn = *we were writing*, etc.

(*c*) By the perfect of baqa with the imperfect of another verb—

baqa yesma' = *he was hearing*
baqêt asma' = *I was hearing*, etc.

(*d*) By the perfect of ṣâr with the imperfect of another verb—

ṣâr yesma' = *he was hearing*, etc.

(iii) *The Present.*

The present sense can be conveyed by:—

(*a*) The use of the active participle, as—

hûwa kâtib = *he is writing*
hîya kâtibe = *she is writing*, etc.

(*b*) The use of 'ammal, 'ammale, 'ammalîn with the imperfect of another verb, thus—

'ammal asma' = *I am hearing*, etc. (see p. 108 above)

(iv) *The Future.*

The future sense can be expressed by—

(*a*) The use of the imperfect of kan with the perfect of another verb, thus—

akûn ketebt = *I shall write*
yekûn keteb = *he will write*
tekûn ketebet = *she will write*, etc.

(*b*) The use of bidd- with personal suffix and the imperfect—

biddi asma‘ = *I shall hear*, etc. (see p. 109 above)

(*c*) The use of the participle râyiḥ with the imperfect, as—

ana râyiḥ asma‘ = *I am going to hear*, etc. (see p. 109 above)

(*d*) In "western" Arabic it is also possible to use the participle mashi in the same way, thus—

mashi yesma‘ = *he will hear*
mashiye tesma‘ = *she is going to hear*, etc.

EXERCISE

(1) kânet raga'et qable ghurûb esh-shems = **She had come before the sunset**

(2) kânû khâdû felûs min et-tuggâr dôl = **They had taken money from those merchants**

(3) eḥna kunna kharagna qabl es-sâ‘a di = **We had gone out before that hour**

(4) kân gâlis hona ‘and abûna = **He was sitting there by the side of our father**

(5) ana kunt sâkin taḥt min en-nâzir = **I was living under the inspector**

(6) êsh râyiḥ te‘mal dilwaqt ? = **What are you going to do now ?**

(7) râyiḥ aq‘ud we-ashrab dukhkhân = **I am going to sit down and smoke**

(8) ana mâshi aq'ud hena ma' el-ustad	= **I am going to sit here with the professor**

(Note: ustad=professor, like French "patron" for the keeper of a restaurant, etc.)

(9) akun ketebt gawâb qable ma akhrug	= **I shall write a letter before I go out**
(10) ente biddek tergi' ila l-beled di we-ḥna biddena neshûfek tâni	= **You will come back to this country again and we shall see you once more**
(11) kêf biddi a'mal ?	= **What shall I do ?**
(12) biddena naṭla' ila barra	= **We must go away**
(13) baqa yesma' kalâm el-ustad	= **He was listening to the words of the professor**

Chapter XX

THE EIGHTEENTH LESSON—USE OF THE PARTICLES

We have already met with and used most of the commoner particles, but it will be well now to make a summary of those in general use. These particles are of use only in sentences which contain either nouns or verbs, or both, though it must be understood that either of these may be implied and not expressed. Thus, if I ask " who has come ? " the answer may be either "Zayd has come ", or " Zayd " alone, and this latter is a complete sentence, because " has come " is implied from the preceding question: so " has Zayd come in ? " receives a complete answer from the verb " he has come in " where the (implied) pronoun refers to Zayd ; it might even receive an answer by the particle " yes " or " no ", though in fact the former means " assuredly " followed by the implied " he has come in ", whilst la = " no " is simply the classical negative " not" (still used in South Arabia) followed by the implied verb. The fact remains that the particles are only used as accessory to nuons and verbs, and they serve to connect words with words or sentences with sentences. Arabic does not possess the mechanical system of punctuation recently developed in written English and the absence of this artificial apparatus makes it the more necessary to connect statements with suitable particles. Thus, we may say written Arabic has to adhere more nearly to the spoken language, and this is true even of the classical speech, because the arrangement and connection of phrases cannot be camouflaged, as in English, by a system of dots and dashes.

The more important particles are of two kinds (i) the prepositions, which connect nouns or verbs with nouns (including noun sentences), some of these prepositions being particles proper, others actual nouns used as prepositions, and (ii) conjunctions which connect nouns with nouns, verbs with verbs, or sentences with sentences.

(i) *Prepositions proper.*

'ala, 'alê- = *upon, against, by*

fât 'alêya	= *he passed by me*
'ala ḥasab	= *according to . . .*
'ala shân, 'ashân (Eg.)	= *because of . . ., in order to . . .*
'ala fikri	= *according to my opinion*
ma 'alêsh	= *no matter*
li ḥaqq 'alêk	= *I have a claim against you*

'an, 'ann- = *from, by*

huwa wâkil 'annuh	= *he is his agent*
sa'al 'an-	= *to enquire about*

'and = *with, in possession of* (see p. 49 above)

kâm 'andek ?	= *what's the time by you ?*
'andek !	= *stop* !
'andek akhbâr ?	= *have you any news ?*

bi- = *by, at, in, with*

er-râgil illi gâlis bi-ganbi	= *the man sitting at my side*
râgil bi-daqn	= *a man with a beard*
aḥsan bi-ketîr	= *much better*
bi-l-lêl	= *by night*

(bi- may thus be used with any noun of time, but it should not be used with a noun of place, unless the place is vague, it might be used for " in the country " but ought not to be used for " in Cairo ".)

bi-llâh = *by God*
(The literary form is wa-llah, the preposition wa- thus used is rare and probably unknown to the un-lettered.)

fi = *in* with nouns of place or time
ḥatta, ḥadd (Eg.) = *up to, until*
ila, ilê- = *to, towards*
ke-, ki- (orig. ka-) = *like*, ki-da (kiza) = *thus*
li- = *to* (owner, recipient, etc.) (see p. 50 above)
gîb li = *give me*
ma' = *with* (see p. 50 above)
ma'ek el-ḥaqq = *you are right*
min, minn- = *from*
sâ'a min dahab = *a watch of gold*
hûwa minnina = *he is one of our party*
tâgir min et-tiggâr = *a certain merchant*
min zamân = *for a long time past*
waṣalni min el-khawâge . . . = *received of Mr. . . .*
matâ = *until* (very rare) (see below. It is now found before verbal sentences and so has become a quasi-conjunction.)

(ii) *Nouns Used as Prepositions.*

ba'd = *after*
ba'di da = *after this*
bên = *between*
bêni we-bênu = *between him and me*
bên el-bênên (dual) = *middling*
fôq = *above*
ghêr = *without* (as negative, see p. 86 above)
khalf = *behind*
misl (mitl) = *like* (very rare in colloquial)
qabl = *before*
ga qabl el-waqt illi . . . = *he came before* (followed by verbal sentence)

qadd = *up to*
taḥt = *under*
wara = *behind*
zêy (Eg.) = *like*
  ezêy = *how ?*
  ezêyek ? = *how are you ?*

A sentence may be equivalent to a noun, thus " fasting is good for you " = " that you fast is good ". Such sentences are often introduced by inn = " indeed ", or ma = " which " (in apposition to the sentence). From this we get the connecting particles—

(*a*) with inn. ghêr inn = *unless*
  'ala inn = *that*
  le-inn = *in order that* or simply *that*
  ma' inn = *although*

(*b*) ma. ba'd ma = *after* (*that*)
  qable ma = *before* (*that*)
  'ashân ma ('ala shân ma) (Eg.) = *because*

(*c*) So ḥatta = *until*
  matâ (with perfect) = *until* (not very common)

Conjunctions

we-, wa-, wi- = " and," connecting words or sentences.
fe-, fa- = " and," connecting sentences with the implication that the second results from or follows after the first.
lâkin, we-lâkin = " but," may take the personal suffixes we-lâkinni = " but I . . ."
amma, we-amma = " but."
aw, ô = " or."
iza, iza kân (as though one word) = " if."
in = " if."

lô, "law" (we-law) = "if" (implying that the condition did not occur, e.g. "if he had come I would have gone out").
lamma = "when."
illa = "unless," "except," illa inn (followed by sentence) = "unless . . ."
mâdâm = "inasmuch as."
ḥatta = "until."
ya . . . y . . . = "either . . . or . . ."
wala . . . wala . . . = "neither . . . nor . . ."

The conjunction we- may be used with iyya (we-iyya, 'Iraq wîya) in the sense of "with", as ruḥ we-iyyah = "go with him," khubz wîya laḥm = "bread with meat" ('Iraq). Really this is the conjunction followed by the accusative case (the "accusative of accompaniment" of the grammarians) and appears in the classical language in such constructions as :—

sîri we-ṭ-ṭarîq musriʿe = *March along the road with haste* (= *march and the road hastening*)

It is not permitted to omit the conjunctions in a series and express the last only, as is done in English, thus "the dog, the ass, and the horse" = el-kelb we-l-ḥimâr we-l-ḥiṣân.

The conjunction we- allows us to introduce a descriptive of the subject or object of a verb, as "I saw him as I was going along the road" = shuftuh we-ana râyîh fi s-sikka (= "I saw him and I was going in the road").

Conditional Sentences

In conditional sentences the "if" clause is introduced by iza, iza kân, or in, or by lô, law, or in if the supposition is improbable or is known not to have happened, and inn, le-inn may be joined to the lô, law. In the literary language the consequence is often introduced by fe-, but this is not common in the colloquial.

iza kunt qâṣid tekteb li- belâd barran = *If you mean to write abroad*
iza kunt ruḥt = *If you had gone*
iza kân yigi = *If he comes*
iza kunte minnek = *If I were you*

Sentences Expressing Cause and Purpose

As already noted it is possible to use a second verb without a connecting particle (cf. p. 108 above), and if the first verb expresses ability, intention, etc., the second naturally introduces the sentence expressing purpose, etc., but very often the purpose is introduced by the preposition li- = " to, for " which thus used governs a sentence instead of a noun.

Notes

" about." The English " about " sometimes means (i) " nearly," as " he came to the mosque about three o'clock " = gâ ila el-gâmi' fi s-sâ'a t-tâlit taqribân (" he came to the mosque at three o'clock nearly "); (ii) " concerning," as istafhim 'alêk = " he enquired about you (concerning you) "; (iii) " about to . . . " implies the future tense, i.e. " going to . . ." (see p. 109 above).

" above." Normally fôq, as eṣ-ṣaṭḥ fôq ed-dâr = " the roof is above the house "; but (i) " above all " = qadâm, (ii) " over and above " = we-'alâwe 'ala da, whilst (iii) " above " often means " more than " and is expressed by the comparative (see p. 91) with min.

" at." Place or time, bi- (not for definitely named places) and fi. E.g. sikit bi-waḥde el-qiriy el-qarîbe min el-Mansûra = " he lives in one of the villages near Mansura." (i) " at " sometimes denotes cause, as " he was astonished at it " = yit'igib minnuh; (ii) " towards " as " he looked at me " = naẓar ilêya; (iii) " with," as " I came at sunrise " = get ma' ṭalû' esh-shems; (iv) " before," as "who is at the door?" = min 'ala l-bâb? (v) "at once" = dilwaqt.

"by." Instrument, time, or place. "By night" = bi-l-lêl (= in the night), "he travelled by steamer" = sâfir fi l-bâbûr (= in the steamer), "I passed by a city" = marrêt bi-medîne. The arithmetical "by" is usually fi = "in", as ralâte fi khamse = "three (multiplied) by five," da talâte amtâr fi arb'a = "that is three metres by four."

"for" sometimes means "to", i.e. the person who is to receive, sometimes "on account of", as el-hamdu li-llâh 'ala da = "praise to God *for* this."

"to," "towards" = ila, so "until", etc.; i.e. in measure of space or time, thus baqêt hona min awwal esh-shahr ila mumtaṣafe = "I stayed there from the first to the middle of the month." "to" sometimes does not denote actual place or time and then often corresponds to 'ala, as izimuh 'ala l-ghadâ = "invite him to dinner." In English "to" often introduces the infinitive which corresponds with the subordinate verb in Arabic, thus "I am not able to hear" = "I am not able (that) I hear". For "to", expressing purpose, see ma aqdirsh asma' above (p. 108).

"from," normally min = "from", relating to time or place, as saqaṭet min îdi = "it fell from my hand," min yôm ila yôm = "from day to day." Sometimes another preposition is implied, as "he dismounted from his horse" = ". . . from upon his horse," nizil min 'ala farasuh. Cause and material are also denoted by min, as sâ'a min dahab = "a watch (made) from gold," but in denoting material the preposition is not necessary, the noun of material can be in apposition (this is true of all the Semitic languages). Note, khadt el-'ilm 'anuh = "I acquired knowledge from him."

" in." Either bi- or fi (see " at " above). " In front of " = amâm, bidlâ min = " instead of . . ." leqêt minnuh asad = " I found in him a lion."

" of." Material (see " from ") as libâsuh min el-ḥarîr = " his garment is of silk." cause (also " from ") huwa mât-min el-kolira = " he died of cholera." amsekûh = " they laid hold of him."

" on," in such as " put on " the " on " is merely due to English idiom, thus ilbas sitrak = " put on your coat " ; sometimes the " on " suggests the Arabic participle as qâbeltûh we-ana dâhib ila bêt = " I met him on my way home " (cf. p. 117) ; we-bi-l-guml'e = " on the whole," sâfar li-yômuh = " he set out on that very day."

" with," instrument bi- as ketebti bi-qalam = " I wrote with a pen," " in company with " = ma' (cf. p. 50), dahab bi-l-lêl = " he went away with the night."

APPENDIX I

CONVERSATION

(i) ORDINARY COURTESIES

A.	salam ‘alêkum	= **Peace be on you**
B.	we-‘alêkum salâm	= **And on you be peace** (*Muslims only*)
A.	nehârkum sa‘îd	= **May our day be prosperous**
B.	nehârkum sa‘îd we-mubârek	= **May your day be prosperous and blessed**
A.	kêf ḥâlkum ?	= **How is your health** (*gazing earnestly at the visitor*)
B.	el-ḥamdu li-llâh	= **Praise be to God**
A.	awḥashtena	= **You have made us lonely** (*not having seen visitor for long*)
B.	Allâh ma yûḥishek	= **May God never let you feel lonely**
A.	(*presenting cup of coffee, first taking sip himself to show that it contains nothing evil*) itfaḍḍal	= **Be pleased**
B.	(*taking the cup*) qahwa dayimân	= **May coffee (be found) for ever (in your house)**
A.	ḍamêt ḥayatek	= **May your vigour continue**
A.	(*after a pause*) tesharraftena	= **You have honoured us**
B.	Allâh yaḥfazek	= **May God preserve you**

(The visitor is careful to sit so that the sole of his foot does not face any of the company. An inferior in the presence of his superior conceals his hands in his sleeves—be careful not to do this in ordinary intercourse. Express no admiration of anything seen as this is the same as asking for it to be given you, nor of any person, child, etc., present—a father would be deeply distressed at hearing any favourable comment on his son and you would be considered responsible for any evil that happened to him. At most say "It is as God wills". If you state what you intend to do in the future be careful to add in shâ'Allâh="if God wills.")

At the end of a visit.

B. khâṭirek *or* 'an iznek = **By your leave**

A. ma'a (ma') s-selâme *or* awaqâtek sa'îde = **(Go) in peace May your times be prosperous**

To a sick man.

ma 'alêk illa l-'âfiye in shâ' allâh.—(*Reply.*)Allâh ye'âfîk = **May there be for thee nothing but health if God will.—God give thee health**

To one who has recovered from illness.

el-ḥamdu li-llâh 'ala l-'âfiye. (*Reply.*) allâh ye'âfîk = **Praise be to God for recovery of health**

When anyone sneezes.

subḥân Allâh *or* el-ḥamdu li-llâh.—(*Reply.*) Allâh yahdîni we-yahdîkum = **Praised be God.—God direct me and you**

After a bath or visit to the barber.

na'imân.—(*Reply.*) Allâh yen'im 'âlêk = **Good favour.—God send good favour on you**

To one starting on a journey.

ṭarîq es-selâme.—(*Reply.*) Allâh yesellinek	= **A journey of peace.—God give you peace**

On return from a journey.

selâmât, ḥamdu li-llâh ‘ala s-salâmât.—(*Reply.*) Allâh yesallimek	= **Greetings. Praise to God for safety.—God save you**

Beggars.

ya muḥannin, ya rabb. *or* li-llâh ya muḥsinîn *or* ya ma ente kerîm, ya rabb., etc. (*Reply to one who begs.*) allâh yeftaḥ ‘alêk *or* Allâh ya‘ṭîk *or* kattar Allâh khayrek, etc.	= **O compassionate, O Lord.—To God, O beneficent.—O how generous art thou, O Lord.—God open upon thee.—God give to thee.—God increase thy favours**

At a feast.

‘îd mubârek ‘alêk	= **May the feast be blessed to you**
(*Reply.*) ‘alêk abrak el-a‘yâd	= **The blessings of festivals for you**

At New Year.

kulli sene we-nte sâlim	= **Every year you in health**
(*Reply.*) we-nte sâlim	= **And you in health**

(ii) At a Hotel or Restaurant

lokânda fên ?	= **Where is there a hotel ?**
di aḥsan lokânda fi l-beled ?	= **Is this the best hotel in the town ?**
mîn ṣâḥib el-lokânda di ?	= **Who is the landlord of this hotel ?**

ya ṣâḥib, fîh ôḍa neḍîfe ? = **Landlord, have you a clean room?**
bi-kam el-ôḍa di ? = **How much is this room?**
da ghâli, khud khamast'âsher qirsh = **That is too dear, take fifteen piastres.**
'andukumshe ḥâḍir li-ghadâ ? = **Have you anything ready for dinner?**
ya walad, kâm ? = **Waiter, how much to pay?**
el-lista fên ? = **Where is the menu?**
da ghâli, ente ghaltân = **That is too much, you have made a mistake.**
ôḍati fên ? = **Where is my room?**
mustorâḥ fên ? = **Where is the W.C.?**

(iii) In a Shop

Shopkeeper. marḥaban bikum, ya khawâge, êsh tinẓur ? = **Welcome, sir, what do you desire?**
Customer. 'andukum sigâgîd ? = **Have you any carpets?**
S. 'andi sigâgîd 'âliye, itfaḍḍal we-ashûfha = **I have carpets of the best quality, please sit down and I will show them**
C. ana 'âwiz es-siggâde di = **I would like this carpet**
S. ṭayyib, ya sîdi, di 'âliye ketîr = **Very well, sir, that is one of excellent quality**
C. qul li nehaytu 'ala âkhir teman = **Tell me what is your lowest price**
S. ifṣil zeye ma ente 'âwiz = **Offer whatever you feel disposed**
C. ente qul li qable tamanha = **You say its price first**
S. bêni we-bên ḥaḍretek tamanha 'ashrîn ginêh bass = **As between me and your honour its price will be twenty pounds, no more**
C. ana addi lek ḥad'âsher = **I would give you eleven**

S. la, yiftaḥ Allâh = **No, God will give me my living**

C. ṭayyib, ḥad'âsher we-nuṣṣ = **Very well, eleven and a half**

S. yerzuq Allâh = **Let God sustain me**

C. ma yaḥteg, âkhir el-kelâm addi lek etn'âsher, ide kunt terîd khud el-felûs, in kân ma terîd fe-wâḥid ghêrek yus'ufni bi-ḥageti = **No matter. My final word is that I will give thee twelve. If thou wilt take the money ; if not, some other than thee will help me in my affair**

S. 'ala khâṭirek, ya tera' teḥsin 'amrek = **At your pleasure. May it be that your business goes prosperously**

C. lêsh te'mal ma'i kida ?—khalleṣek etn'âsher we-nuṣṣ ? = **Why act with me thus ?—Would twelve and a half satisfy thee ?**

S. ya akhi, ma teq'udshe tinâkifni: balâsh menakfa. Da mush shira di illi ente tishtirîh = **My brother, do not continue to worry me. Enough of annoyance. That is not the way for you to do business**

C. khalleṣek telât'âsher ? = **Would thirteen satisfy thee ?**

S. 'ase turîd hidîya minni = **Perhaps you expect a present from me**

C. la, kêf da hidîya ?—khalleṣek telât'âsher we-nuṣṣ ? = **No, how can it be a present ? —Would thirteen and a half satisfy ?**

S. ṭayyib, aqul ya ma yi'awwaḍ. Allâh yikassibek hât el-felûs. khaṣrân kasbân, nihaitu ḥadiḥna. bi'na we-s-selâm = **All right. I will say, How great is he who consoles. May God give thee profit. Hand over the money ; loss or gain in what we have sold, that is the end of the matter**

(iv) Military

imshi li-qudâm. ‘andek	= **March. Halt**
li-qudâm. inzil	= **Forward. Dismount**
sallim nefsek. irmi silâhek	= **Surrender. Lay down your arms**
ma takhâfûsh, eḥna ‘asâkir inkelîzi	= **Do not be afraid, we are English soldiers**
shêkh el-beled fên ?	= **Where is the head man of the village**
hâtuh hêna	= **Bring him here**
‘andukum min el-khêl kam râs ?	= **How many horses have you ?**
nedfa‘ lek neqdiye li-l-kull	= **I will pay cash for everything**
in ma gama‘tûsh el-kull fi sâ‘atên arsil lekum ‘asâkari	= **If you do not collect everything in two hours I will send my soldiers**
qul bi-l-ḥaqq, ma tikdibsh	= **Speak the truth, tell no lies**
we-ma takhfîsh el-hâga fa-yesîr sharra lukum	= **And do not hide anything or it will be the worse for you**
akhad el-kull we-addi lek bîh waṣl	= **I will take everything and give you a receipt**
ma takhafsh, lek el-felûs bala shakk	= **Do not be afraid, you will be paid without fail**
ente mahzum ?	= **Are you a deserter ?**
emta farart ?	= **When did you escape ?**
min ên farart ?	= **Where did you escape from ?**
el-qarâwul fên ?	= **Where are the outposts ?**

APPENDIX II

THE CALL TO PRAYER

Allâh akbar	= **God is greatest**

(Twice repeated in Malikite rite in Upper Egypt and Africa generally, except Lower Egypt; in other rites four times repeated.)

ashhad an lâ ilâh illa -llâh we-Muhammad rasûl Allâh (*twice*)	= **I testify that there is no god save God and that Muhammad is the apostle of God**
ḥayy ila ṣ-ṣalât, ḥayy ila l-felâḥ (*twice*)	= **Up to prayer, up to salvation**
eṣ-ṣalât khêr min en-nûm (*twice*)	= **Prayer is better than sleep**
Allâh akbar	= **God is greatest** (*twice*)
lâ -llâh illa -llâh	= **There is no god but God** (*once*)

APPENDIX III

SÛRATU L-FÂTIḤAH

(In colloquial Arabic we are not, of course, concerned with the classical forms of literature, still less with theology, which for the most part the foreigner will be wise to leave alone unless some Muslim starts the subject. Still it will not be inappropriate to take this one passage, the first *sûra* or section of the Qur'an which is used by Muslims very much as the Lord's Prayer is used by Christians and will often be seen used in ornamental inscriptions: it is recited together by two merchants when they have concluded a bargain and figures prominently on many other occasions, besides which phrases from it will be recognized as appearing in various salutations, etc. The Arabic is, of course, classical in form and hardly intelligible to the average uneducated fellaḥ, so in the notes various grammatical remarks and rules appear which will be unfamiliar to the learner.)

(The heading "Sûratu l-Fâtiḥah" means "section of the opening", the final -u in Sûratu is the classical nominative termination: the -at preceding will be recognized as the feminine termination used before the genitive (cf. sect. 26), the word appears in the Dictionary as Sura.)

(1) Bismi-llâhi r-Raḥmâni r-Raḥîm = *In the name of God the Compassionate, the Merciful*

bi- = "in," then -(i)sm = "name" with -i added for the classical genitive which has to follow the preposition. r-Raḥmân = "the Compassionate," the article assimilated to the following R, and the -i added as mark of the genitive; r-Raḥîm = "the Merciful," again the article assimilated, but this time no added -i because the final short vowels for case or mood are dropped at the pause which ends a verse. (Muslims of the orthodox type do not have pictures in their houses and you will often see this verse, sometimes in a peasant's hut beautifully written in white chalk on the mud wall. The verse is commonly used as an exclamation on seeing anything extraordinary, and as an invocation before commencing any undertaking.)

(2) Al-ḥamdu li-llâhi Rabbi l-'âlamîn = *Praise to God, Lord of the worlds*

ḥamd = " praise," with the nominative ending -u ; li-llâhi = " to God," with genitive -i after the preposition ; Rabbi = " Lord " with gen. -i to agree with -llâhi ; l-'âlamîn = " of the worlds " genitive plural (strong).

(3) 'ar-Raḥmâni r-Raḥîm = *The compassionate, the merciful*

Both genitives to agree with the -llâhi preceding, but gen. -i not with the second as it comes at the pause which ends the verse.

(4) Mâliki yômi d-dîn = *King of the day of judgment*

Mâliki, gen. with -i still in agreement with -llâhi ; yômi gen., governed by Mâliki, d-dîn gen. in iḍafat (see p. 82), but the -i omitted at pause.

(5) 'Iyyâka na'budu wa-'iyyâka nasta'în = *Thee do we worship and thee do we ask for help*

Instead of using the pronominal suffix in the usual way (p. 40) the emphatic particle 'iyyâ- with the suffixed pronoun is placed in front of the verb, this conveys exceptional emphasis. na'budu = " we worship," verb 'abad, hence 'abdullâh = " slave of God," the -u at the end of the verb is the classical termination of the indicative mood.

wa-'iyyâka nasta'în = "and thee do we ask for help," (i)st = Ct. form of the verb 'ân (medial w, i.e. root 'wn), but indicative -u not added at the end of a verse: in classical Arabic both the short vowels for the cases of nouns and those for the moods of verbs are dropped in "pause", i.e. at a full stop.

(6) ihdinâ ṣ-ṣirâṭa l-mustaqîm

ihdinâ = "guide us"; ṣ-ṣirâta-l-mustaqîm = "(in) the way of the upright."

(7) ṣirâṭa-llâdhîna 'an'amta 'alayhim ghayri l-maghḍûbi 'alayhim wa-lâ ḍ-ḍâllîn

ṣirâṭa-llâdhîna = "the way of those who," (a)llâdhîna is the full classical form of the relative which colloquial speech shortens to illi. 'an'amta 'alayhim = "thou hast bestowed on them," class. -ta in 2nd sing. of perfect where colloquial has -t. "Those who thou hast bestowed on them" = "those on whom thou hast bestowed." In class. speech -hum becomes -him by assimilation to the preceding -y-. ghayri l-maghḍûbi 'alayhim = "not (those who have) wrath upon them"; lit. "other than those . . ." (ghayr as negative). wa-lâ = "nor," la in class. Arabic is used simply for "not", as it still is in Oman and other southern parts but in Egypt, Syria, etc., it survives only as "no". ḍ-ḍâllîn = "(those who) go astray".

Appendix IV

THE ALGERIAN DIALECT

(Notes for tourists, etc., in Algeria, Morocco, etc.)

The Arabic of the West (Maghrabi, i.e. Algeria, Morocco, etc.) is not a different language, but has some dialectal peculiarities which at first make it appear very different from the Arabic of Egypt and Syria but on closer scrutiny simply show certain clearly defined tendencies which can be mastered without much difficulty.

The key to these differences is the accent. In Egypt, Syria, and to a great extent in 'Iraq, the accent of stress recedes from the end of the word until it falls upon a long vowel or upon a short followed by two consonants, thus :—

áḥmar, béled, kéteb,

as no syllable has a long vowel or double closure the accent recedes to the first syllable,

ḍarábt, ḍarábtu, ḍárabu, ḍárabet, gedíd

in the first two of these the accent goes back until it rests upon a short followed by two consonants, in the third it goes back without finding a double closure or long (as the final long is not counted), and so in the fourth word : in the last the -í- is long so the accent goes back no further.

The older accent was free and was not controlled by long vowels or double closure and this older usage survives in the western Arabic, thus beléd, ketéb, etc., and the tendency is to drop or slur over the short vowel preceding the accent, and so we get Algerian, Tunisian, and Moroccan qtél, ktéb, bléd, etc., for qétel, kéteb, béled. So áḥmar becomes ḥmár, áḥad becomes ḥád (cf. "eleven" = ḥad'asher on p. 73), akal becomes kál and akhad becomes khád (p. 132), etc. That this change has taken place in the colloquial of Egypt, Syria, etc., as in those instances just noted, shows that there also the accent once was free as in Maghrabi; it would have been impossible to drop the accented syllable. It is this difference of accent, which at first makes the western Arabic seem so strange, but bearing in mind (i) that the accent is free and varies in position, often getting on the last syllable, and (ii) that a short vowel before the accent is generally hurried over, very often omitted altogether, we find that this western speech offers no serious difficulties. The following examples will indicate the characteristic differences :—

Verb.	Perfect.	ktíbt (ktíbit)	= *I wrote, thou didst write*
		ktíbti	= *thou* (fem.) . . .
		ktíb	= *he wrote*
		ktíbna	= *we wrote*
		ktíbtu	= *you wrote*
		kítbu	= *they wrote*

Imperfect, both positions of accent are in use, thus either—

yíktib	or	yiktíb,
tíktib		tiktíb,
tíktebi		t'kítebi (2nd fem. sing.)

Pronoun	ána	or	aná,
	énta	or	entá, etc.

ṣbaḥ el-khair	= *Good morning*
t'bark Allâh	= *Bless God*
el-qalîl min el-ḥabîb katîr	= *Little from a friend is much*

el-ʿabd yámmel wa-r-rabb ikímmel = *The slave plans, and the Lord carries out* (cf. p. 130)
kull shi fi yad Allâh = *Everything is in God's hands* (cf. p. 90)

The Kabyle, Rif mountaineers, etc., are Berbers and speak the Berber language, which is distinct from Arabic. In some districts (e.g. Tlemsen in Algeria) where there is contact with the Berbers very often *t* (th) is pronounced like *ts*, thus k'tsébts "I wrote" (= ketebt), k'tseb "he wrote", etc., but these peculiarities are hardly likely to be met with by the ordinary traveller.

VOCABULARY

Nouns

Some of the rarer words which occur in the examples are not included here. The notes (E), (S), (I) denote words peculiar to the dialects of Egypt, Syria, or ‘Iraq respectively. When alternative forms differ only in the dental aspirate dh, or th, the aspirated form is that used in ‘Iraq, the non-aspirate that in Syria and Egypt. The sign (*) denotes words in -a, -e, which make -at, -et before a suffix, etc. (Cf. p. 41 above.) In all cases the q commonly appears as ‘ in Lower Egypt, etc., and g in ‘Iraq and Upper Egypt. The forms in parentheses are the plurals.

ablution	= wuḍu‘
account	= ḥisâb (-ât)
address	= ‘anwin
afternoon	= ‘aṣr
age	= ‘umr
agent	= wakîl
air	= hawa
almond	= gôz
animal	= ḥiwân (-ât)
ant	= namle* (naml)
apostle	= rasûl (rosol). The proper title for Muhammad is rasûl allâh = “Apostle of God”
apricot	= mishmish
arrival	= wiṣûl, wuṣûl
ass	= ḥimâr (ḥemîr)
automobile	= otomôbîl
bag	= shanṭa* (shonaṭ)
baker	= khabbâz
banana	= môze* (môz)
bank (for money)	= bank (benûk)
barber	= ḥallâq
barley	= shi‘îr
basin	= ṭisht (ṭeshût)
basket	= miqtaf
bat	= weṭâṭ (waṭawîṭ)
bath	= ḥammâm
beans	= fûl
beard	= daqn (fem.)
bed	= farsh
bee	= naḥle* (naḥl)
beetle	= khunfuse* (khunfus)
bird (*large*)	ṭêra* (ṭêr); (*small*) ‘aṣfûre* (‘aṣfûr)
blanket	= ḥirâm (iḥrima)
blessing	= varke*
blood	= damm
book	= kitâb (kutub)
boot	= gazma* (gizâm)
box	= ṣandûq
boy	= walad (wilâd awlâd)
bread	= ‘êsh (E.); khubz
breakfast	= fuṭur
bride	= ‘arûse* (‘arâyes)

bridegroom = 'aris (arâyes)
bridge = qantara*
broker = simsâr
brother = akh, akhû- (ekhwâ, ikhwân)
bud = zer-ward
buffalo = gamûse* (gamûs)
bug = baqqa*
bull = tôr, thôr (tîrân)
burden = ḥiml, ḥuml
business = shughl
cab = 'arba*
cabbage = koronb
calf = 'egl ('egûl)
camel = gemel (gimâl)
camp = mu'asker
canal = tir'a (tera')
carpenter = naggâr
carrier = ḥammâl
cat = quṭṭa* (-ât)
catalogue = katâlôg
cauliflower = qarnabît
chair = kursi
chauffeur = shôfer
cheque = shakk
chicken = katkût (katakît)
child = ṭifl (aṭfâl)
cholera = kutêra*
church = kinîsa*
cigarette = sigâra*
city = medîna*
class = darage*
cloud = ghêm (gheyûm)
clothes (see *garment*)
coffee (*drink*) qahwa ; (*berry*) bunn
coin = 'umla*
colic = maghṣ
colour = lawn, lôn (ilwân)
comb = mesht (amshâṭ)
condition = ḥâl
conduct = tadbîr, sîra*
constipation = ensâk
consul = qonṣul
consumption = sill
cook = ṭabbâkh
copper = naḥâs
coppersmith = naḥḥâs
corn = qamḥ
cotton = quṭn
cough = kuḥḥa*

country = beled (bilâd)
cover = ghaṭâ
cow = baqara* (baqar)
crops = zirâ'ât
cucumber = khêyâr
cup = fingân
cupboard = dûlâb
custom = 'âda
cut-purse = neshtar (Turk.)
danger = khâṭir
daughter = bint
dawn = fagr
day = yôm (iyâm) ; nehâr
day-break = fagr
death = môt
deer = ghazal (ghozlan)
desert = ṣaḥrâ (ṣaḥâri)
devil = shêṭân ; 'ifrîṭ
diarrhœa = eshâl
dinner = ghadâ
divorce = ṭalâq
dog = kelb (kilâb)
dollar = riyâl (-ât)
door = bâb (ibwâb)
dove = ḥamâma* (-ât)
dung = zibl
dust = ṭurâb
ear = widn (fem.)
earth = arḍ (fem.) (arâḍî)
egg = bêḍa* (bêḍ)
electricity = kahrabaiya, lekterik
elephant = fîl
evening = mesâ
examination = emteḥân
exercise = dars
eye = 'ên
face = wishsh
family = ahl
fare = ugre*
farm = 'azba*
fast = ṣûm
father = ab, abû-
favour = faḍla*
fear = khôf
feast = 'îd
fever = ḥumma*
field = ghêṭ (ghîṭân)
field mouse = girdôn

fig = tîn
figure = raqam (arqâm)
file = mabrad
fire = nâr
fish = samaka* (samak)
fishing = ṣêd
fisherman = ṣayyâd
flat (*apartment*) = ṭabaqe*
flower = ẓahr (ẓuhûr)
fly = debbâne*
follower = tâbî' (-în)
foot = rigl
fowl = farkha* (firâkh)
fox = ta'lab, tha'lab (ta'aleb)
friend = ṣâḥib
fruit = tamar
garden = genîne* (ganâyen); bustân (Pers.)
garment = libâs
garlic = tôm, thôm
gazelle = ghazâl (ghozlân)
gentleman = khawâge
gipsy = nawâri
girl = bint
glass = kubbaya*, fingân
goat = me'za* (-ât)
God = Allah, -llâh
gold = dahab
goose = wizza* (-ât)
government = ḥukm
governor = ḥâkim, wali, mudîr
grapes = 'inab
grass = hashish
groom = sâ'is, sâyis
gun = bunduqîye*
hair = sha'r (she'ûr)
hairbrush = fûrsha* (forash)
half = nuṣṣ
hammer = metraqa* (matâreq)
hand = yêd, îd
handkerchief = mandîl
harm = sharr
hat = burnêṭa* (barânîṭ)
hay = derîs
head = râs
heat = ḥarr
hell = gehennem
hill = tell
holiday = fusḥa*
honey = 'asl
horse = ḥiṣân
hotel = lôkânda*
hour = sâ'a*
house = bêt (biyût); dâr (fem.) (diyar)
hunting = ṣêd
hunter = ṣayyâd
husband = zôg
ink = ḥebr
inn = khân (Pers.)
inspector = nâẓir
intelligence = 'aql
iron = ḥadîd
island = gezîra* (gezâyer)
jackal = ibn âwa
jaw = fakk (fekûk)
judge = qâḍi
jug = ibrîq
key = miftâḥ (mafâtîḥ)
king = melek (mulûk)
knife = sikkîn
knowledge = 'ilm
lamb = kharûf (kherfân)
lamp = sirag
land = arḍ
lead = roṣṣâṣ
left (*hand*) = shemâl
lemon = lemûna* (lemûn)
lesson = dars
letter = mektûb (mekâtîb); gawâb (-ât)
lettuce = khass
liberty = ḥurrîye*
life = ḥiya* (existence); nefs (soul); sîra*
light = nâr
lightning = barq
lion = asad
locusts = garâd
lord = sayyid
luggage = 'afsh
lung = riyya* (-ât)
lupine = tirmis

magazine (storehouse) = makhzen
maize = durra*
majesty = galâla*
man = râgil (rigâl); *mankind*, nâs; *old man*, shêkh, 'agûz (Eg.)
manners = 'adâb
mare = faras (afrâs)
market = sûq
marriage = zawâg
measles = ḥaṣba*
meat = lahm
medicine = dawâ (adwiyâ)
melon = shammâm
merchant = tâgir (tiggâr)
middle = wasṭ
might = qûwa
mile = mîl
milk = leven, ḥaleb
minister = wazîr
minute = deqîqa* (daqâyeq)
money = felûs
money-changer = ṣarrâf
monkey = qerd (qerûd)
morning = ṣabâh, ṣubḥ
morsel = luqma*
mosque = gâmi', mesgid
mosquito = namûse* (namûs)
mother = umm
mountain = gebel (gibâl)
mouse = fâr (firân)
moustaches = shanab (ashnâb)
mouth = famm (afmâm)
mud = ṭîn
mule = baghl, -e* (beghâl)
nail = mesmâr (mesâmîr)
name = ism
negro = ḥabeshi
neighbour = gâr, gâriye*
news = khabar (akhbâr)
night = lêl. lêle*
noon = dohr, ẓohr
nose = anf (enuf)
number = 'adad
officer = ẓâbiṭ (ẓubbâṭ)
oil = zêt
olive = zêtûn
onion = baṣal
opinion = fikr
opportunity = furṣa*
orange = bortuqân
owl = bûma* (-ât)
ox = tôr, thôr (tîrân)
page (of book) = wagh (awgoh)
pain = waga'
palace = qaṣr (quṣur)
palm (tree) = nakhl, nakhle* (single tree)
paper = waraq (awrâq)
parent = wâlid
passport = teskari
peace = salâm, salâme*
pen = qalam
permission = idhn, idn, izn
petrol = gâz (E.), ghâz (S.I.)
physician = ḥakîm
piastre = qirsh (qurûsh)
pig = khanzîr (khanazîr)
pigeon = ḥamâma (-ât)
pilgrimage = ḥagg
piper = zammân
place = maṭraḥ, mekân
plague = ṭâ'ûn
plant = nabât (-ât)
plate = ṣaḥn (ṣuḥûn)
play = le'ab
police = bûlîṣ
pond = birka*
porter = ḥammâl
postman = sâ'î bûsṭa
post office = bûsṭa*
potato = baṭâṭes
pound (money) ginêh (-ât); *(weight)* raṭl
power = qûwa
praise = ḥamd
prayer = ṣala
price = taman, si'r
prison = ḥabs, sign
promise = wa'd
property = mâl
prophet = nabi
pupil = talmîd

purgative = sharba*
quantity = qadd
quince = safargel
railway = sikket el-ḥadîd
rain = maṭar
rat = fâr (firân)
religion = dîn
remainder = baqi
rice = ruzz
right (hand) = yemin
ring = rann
river = nahr
road = ṭarîq
roof = ṣaṭḥ
room = ôḍa
rope = ḥabl
rug = busâṭ (absiṭa)
saddle = sarg
saddlebag = khurg (khurag)
salt = malḥ
sample = namûna (namâyin); 'êniyye*
sand = raml
school = medrese*
scorpion = 'aqrab ('aqâreb)
screw = qalawûz (-ât)
sea = baḥr
seeds = bizr
self = nefs
servant = khaddâm
sesame = semsem
shade = ẓall
sheep = ghanam
ship = markib
shop = dukkân
shore = shâṭi (shawâṭi)
shoulder = kitf
silk = ḥarîr
silver = faḍḍa
sister = ukht
sky = samâ'
slave = 'abd, 'ebd
sleep = nâm
small-pox = gidrî
smith = haddâd
smoke = dukhkhân
snail = ḥalazûn
snake = tu'bân, thu'bân
snow = ṭalg
soap = sabûn
soldier = 'askari
son = ibn (awlâd, abnâ)
soup = shorba*
speech = kelâm
spider = 'ankabût
spirit = rûḥ (arwâḥ)
sponge = isfenge* (ât)
spoon = mal'aqa* (malâ'eq)
spring (*of water*), 'ayn ('uyûn); (*season*) rabî'
star = negm (nugum); kawkab (kawâkib)
state = ḥâl
station (*railway*) muḥaṭṭa*; *station-master*, nâzir el-muḥaṭṭa
steamer = wâbûr
stick = 'aṣâ ('uṣî)
stomach = baṭn (beṭûn)
stone = ḥagar (aḥgâr)
storm = zôba'a* (zawâbe')
street = shâri' (shawâri'); hara*
sugar = sukkar
sugar-cane = qaṣab
summer = ṣêf
sun = shems
sunset = maghrub
supper = 'ashâ
sword = sêf
tail = dîl, dhîl (deyûl)
tailor = khayyâṭ
tamarisk = ṭarfâ, ṭarfe*
task = shughl
tea = shay
teacher = mu'allim
telegraph = tiligrâf
thief = ḥarâmi (ḥarâm)
thought = fikr
ticket = teskari
time = zemam (azmâm); waqt (awqât)
tobacco = dukhkhân
tomato = ṭamâṭem
tongue = lisân (alsina)
tooth = sinne* (sinn)
town = beled (bilâd), cf. *city*

traveller = musâfir
tree = shagare* (eshgâr)
truth = ḥaqq
vacation = fusḥa*
village = qarya* (qaraya)
vine = karm (kerûm)
vineyard = karm ʻinab
virgin = bekr (bukûr)
voice = ṣôt (aṣwât)
watch = sâʻa* (-ât)
wasp = dabbûr (dababîr)
water = môya
wealth = mâl
weather = hawa
week = gumʻa* (gumaʻ)
well (*of water*) = bîr (abyâr)
widow = armale* (arâmel)
wife = zôga* (zôgât)
wind = rîḥ (aryâḥ)
window = shebbâk (shabâbîk)
wine = nebît
winter = shetâ
woman = mara (nesâ); *old woman*, ʻaguz (ʻagâyez), ʻaguze* (E.)
wood = khashab
wool = ṣûf
world = dunya
worm = dûde* (dûd)
year = sena* (senîn)
young man = shâbb (shubbân)

ADJECTIVES

alive = ḥaiy
angry = zaʻlân (2)
bad = radi (3)
beloved = ḥabîb (1)
black = aswad (4)
blessed = mubârak
blind = aʻma (5)
blue = azraq (4)
broad = ʻarîḍ (1)
cheap = rakhîs (1)
cheerful = farḥân (2)
civilized = mutemodin
cold = bârid (of things); bardân (of persons) (2)
complete = tamm
crafty, cunning = shaṭîr (1)
dear (*beloved*) = ʻazîz (1), (price) ghâli (3)
dead = mêyit
deaf = akhraṣ (5)
deep = ghawît (1)
difficult = ṣaʻab
distant = baʻîd (1)
dumb = akhras (5)
foolish = ghashîm (1)
forbidden = ḥarâm
generous = kerîm (1)
good = ṭayyib-khêr
great (*in size*) = kebîr (1) (in power, dignity), ʻaẓîm (1)
green = akhdar (4)
happy = mesrur, mabsuṭ (7)
hard = ṣaʻb, ṣaʻab
heavy = tigîl (1)
high = ʻali (3)
honest = ṣâliḥ (6)
hot = ḥarr
hungry = gûʻân (2)
idle (see *lazy*)
ignorant = gâhil (6)
ill = marîḍ (1)
intelligent = ʻâqil (6)
lame = aʻrag (5)
lazy = keslân (2)
light = sahil
little = qelîl (1)
long = ṭawîl (1)
much = ketîr (1)
neighbouring = qarîb (1)
new = gedîd (1)
old = qadîm (1)
open = meftûḥ (7)
original = aṣli (3)
poor = faqîr (1)
present = ḥaḍîr (1)

pretty = leṭîf (1), kuwayis
prosperous = sa'îd (1)
ready (see *present*)
red = aḥmar (4)
reliable = ṣâliḥ (6)
rich = ghani (3)
short = qasîr (1)
skilful = mâhir (6)
small = ṣaghîr (1), sughayir
soft = nâ'im (6)
spacious = wâsi' (6)
standing = qâyim (6)
stoned (*of the devil*) = ragîm (1)
straight = dughri (3)
strong = qawî (1)
suitable = ṭalîq (1)
sweet = ḥolw
thirsty = 'aṭshân (2)
tired = ta'bân (2)
untrustworthy = qabîḥ (1)
upright = ṣâdiq (6)
useful = nâfi', mufid
violent = shedîd (1)
watchful = neshîṭ (1)
weak = da'îf (1)
wet = meblûl (7)
white = abyaḍ (4)
wise = 'ârif, 'âlim (6)
yellow = safra (4)

(1) These are adjectives of the qatîl type, fem. qatîle*.
(2) Type qatlân.
(3) Adjectives with final -i.
(4) Adjectives of colour, see p. 92.
(5) Adjectives of bodily defect, see p. 93.
(6) Active participles of verbs.
(7) Passive participles.

Verbs

(The letters in parentheses denote the vowels in the imperfect-imperative. D, D*, Dt, etc., denote the derived stems (cf. p. 131) (I), (II), (III) show verbs weak in first, second, or third radicals respectively, whilst (MG) denotes those with second and third consonants alike.)

able, to be = qadar (i)
appear = ṭala' (u)
arise = qâm (II)
arrive = waṣal (i) (I)
ask (*question*) = sa'al (a)
ask for = ṭalab
avert = gall (MG)
awake = ṣaḥḥ (MG)
be = kân (II), ṣâr (II, in sense of "continue")
bear ḥame=
begin = qam (II)
break = kasar (a)
bring (*a thing*), gâb (II); *person*, ḥaḍḍir (D)
buy = ishtara (st, III)
can (see *be able*)
carry out = kemmil (D)
close = naffed (D) (II, III)
come = gâ, ta'âla, ta'al (imperat.)
compel = khallâ (III, D)
concern = khaṣṣ (MG)
converse = tekellim (Dt)

continue = baqâ (III)
count = ‘add (MG)
descend = nizil, ḥall (MG)
die = mât (II), wafî (III)
dispute = tefattish (Dt)
dizzy, to be = dâḥ (II)
do = ‘amal (a)
drink = shirib
eat = kal (I)
empty, be = faragh
enquire = istafahim (st)
enter = dakhel
fast = ṣâm (II)
fear = khâf (II)
finish = khaliṣ
forget = nesâ (III)
found, be = wagad (I)
free, be = fadâ (III)
give = ‘aṭâ (III), iddâ (III)
go = râḥ (II), mishî (III)
go down = nizil
go away = kharag
guide = hadâ (III)
handcuff = kalabsh (Turk.)
happen = haṣal
hear = sami‘ (a)
hot, be = ḥarr (MG)
humiliate = dâkh (II)
increase = zâd (II)
journey = sâfir (D*)
knock = khabbiṭ (D)
know = ‘arif (i)
laugh = daḥak
learn = te‘allam (Dt)
learn by heart = ḥafaẓ
lengthen = ṭawwil (II, D)
like = ḥabb (MG)
live = ‘âsh (II)
load = ḥammil (D)
measure = kâl (II)
meet = laqâ (III)
mount = rekeb
must = lazim
need = ‘âz (II)
obliged, be (see *must*)
open = fataḥ (a)
overtake = lahaq
pass by = fât (II)
pick up = lamm (i) (MG)
pilgrimage, go on = ḥagg (MG)
plan = ‘ammil (D)
pleased, to be = tefaḍḍil (Dt)
pray = ṣallâ (III)
present, to be = ḥaḍer (a)
preserve = saḥim (III)
profit = hanî (III)
read = qarâ (III)
reckon = ḥasab (u)
reduce = naqaṣ
refuge, to take = ‘âd (II)
return = raga‘ (i)
run away = garâ (III)
safe, to be = salam
satisfied, to be = shabi‘
save = sallim (D)
say = qâl (II)
see = shâf (II)
seek = ṭalab (u)
seize = misik
send = rasal (i)
shut = qafal (u)
silent, to be = seket (u)
stretch out = madd (III)
strike = ḍarab (a)
stroll = tefessaḥ (Dt)
suppose = ẓann (MG)
sweep = kenes
take = khad (= akhad)
talk = kalam
teach = ‘allam (D)
tell = khabbir (D)
understand = fahim (a)
visit = shaqq (MG)
waste = ṣaraf
will (of God) = shâ’ (II)
write = keteb (u)

خنیمر لاورد

مایثث